Study Guide With Map

for use with

The Unfinished Nation

A Concise History of the American People

Volume Two: From 1865

Third Edition

Alan Brinkley

Columbia University

Prepared by
Harvey H. Jackson III
Jacksonville State University

Bradley R. Rice
Clayton College & State University

Boston   Burr Ridge, IL   Dubuque, IA   Madison, WI   New York   San Francisco   St. Louis
Bangkok   Bogotá   Caracas   Lisbon   London   Madrid
Mexico City   Milan   New Delhi   Seoul   Singapore   Sydney   Taipei   Toronto

McGraw-Hill Higher Education

A Division of The McGraw-Hill Companies

Study Guide with Map Exercises for use with
THE UNFINISHED NATION: A CONCISE HISTORY OF THE AMERICAN PEOPLE,
VOLUME TWO: FROM 1865, THIRD EDITION

1 2 3 4 5 6 7 8 9 0 BKM/BKM 9 0 3 2 1 0 9

ISBN 0-07-235975-7

www.mhhe.com

ABOUT THE AUTHORS

Harvey H. Jackson received his Ph.D. from the University of Georgia. With Bradley R. Rice, he wrote *Georgia: Empire State of the South*. He authored or coauthored books on early America, including *Lachlan McIntosh and the Politics of Revolutionary Georgia* (1979), and is now focusing his studies on the cultural environment of the South. In 1995 he published *Rivers of History: Life on the Coosa, Tallapoosa, Cahaba, and Alabama*, and in 1997 he published *Putting 'Loafing Streams' to Work: The Building of Lay, Mitchell, Martin and Jordan Dams, 1910–1929*. Jackson is currently working on a study of the northern coast of the Gulf of Mexico since World War II. His articles have appeared in several anthologies and journals including the *Journal of Southern History* and the *William and Mary Quarterly*. Harvey Jackson is Professor and Head of the Department of History and Foreign Languages at Jacksonville State University, Jacksonville, Alabama.

Bradley R. Rice received his Ph.D. from the University of Texas at Austin. He coauthored *Georgia: Empire State of the South* with Harvey H. Jackson and wrote *Progressive Cities: The Commission Government Movement in America, 1901–1920* (1977). Rice is coauthor and coeditor of *Sunbelt Cities: Politics and Growth Since World War II* (1983), and his work has appeared in several edited collections and journals including the *Journal of Urban History*. Since 1982, Rice has been editor of
Atlanta History: A Journal of Georgia and the South, which is published quarterly by the Atlanta Historical Society. Rice is Professor of History and Assistant Vice President for Academic Affairs at Clayton College & State University, Morrow, Georgia.

TABLE OF CONTENTS

Introduction

Every history professor has heard hundreds of students complain that history is nothing but dry, irrelevant facts, names, and dates to be memorized quickly and just as quickly forgotten. To be sure, for students to have a good framework of historical understanding, they must have a basic knowledge of factual information, but history is much more than that. Names and dates are really people and time. History is society's memory, and society cannot function without history any more than an individual could function without his or her memory. The names represent real flesh-and-blood people, both famous and common, and the dates mark the time when those people lived and worked. This study guide will try to lead you toward developing a historical perspective. You will be encouraged to go beyond the bare facts to think critically about the causes and consequences of historical decisions. Careful study of this guide in consultation with your instructor will help you use the text to its best advantage. With the guide, you can constantly test yourself to make sure that you have learned from what you have read.

Each chapter of the guide is composed of several parts: Objectives, Pertinent Questions, Identification, Document, Map Exercise, Summary, and a Self-Test. Your instructor may assign specific items from the guide that best complement his or her approach to the course, or you may be expected to use the guide on your own. It will work well with either approach. The guide is not a workbook or a shortcut. It does not recapitulate, outline, or simplify the work of Professor Brinkley. Rather, it is designed to challenge you to seek a better comprehension of the text in particular and American history in general.

It is best to look over the appropriate chapter in the guide before you read your assignment so that you will be better attuned to what to look for as you read. The objectives that are listed at the beginning of each chapter of the study guide will give you a general idea of what the chapter is about. The Identification items are important names and terms covered in the text but not usually directly mentioned in the Pertinent Questions section of the study guide. Of course, your instructor may add to and/or delete from these lists to meet the needs of the course.

The Pertinent Questions and the Self-Test questions are the heart of the study guide. The goal of these exercises is to provide you with a thoughtful method for self-assessment after you have read each chapter. Some students will wish to write out their answers in full; some will jot down a few key ideas; and others will simply check themselves "in their heads." Experiment and use whichever method works best for you (assuming it is acceptable to your instructor). You should keep in mind that no general survey text could possibly cover all the pertinent questions in American history or fully explicate those it does discuss. Do not become too preoccupied with incidental supporting detail. Look for the essence of the answer, and then seek out those facts and examples that support your conclusions.

The Document exercises in each chapter provide an opportunity for you to discover how important the analysis of documents can be to the historian's task. The questions about each document should be treated much like the Pertinent Questions. The Map Exercises let you see how geography can help you form a historical perspective.

At the end of the guide are sections that will help you write a critical book review or research paper if your instructor so requires. Such assignments will give you the opportunity to exercise critical thinking skills and apply the historical perspective that you have cultivated while reading the text and using this guide.

Naturally, this all seems like a drawn-out process, and at first it may well be. But as you work at it, you will find that each chapter will take less time, until finally you will have developed a system of study habits and analysis that will serve you well in this course and in many others as well.

Harvey H. Jackson
Bradley R. Rice

Reconstruction and the New South

CHAPTER FIFTEEN

Reconstruction and the New South

OBJECTIVES

A thorough study of Chapter 15 should enable you to understand:

1. The conditions in the former Confederacy after Appomattox that would have made any attempt at genuine reconstruction most difficult.

2. The differences between the Conservative and Radical views on the reconstruction process, and the reasons for the eventual Radical domination.

3. The functioning of the impeachment process in the case of President Andrew Johnson, and the significance of his acquittal for the future of Reconstruction.

4. Radical Reconstruction in practice, and Southern (black and white) reaction to it.

5. The debate among historians concerning the nature of Reconstruction, its accomplishments, and its harmful effects on the South.

6. The national problems faced by President Ulysses S. Grant, and the reasons for his lack of success as chief executive.

7. The diplomatic successes of the Johnson and Grant administrations, and the role of the presidents in achieving them.

8. The greenback question, and how it reflected the postwar financial problems of the nation.

9. The alternatives that were available during the election of 1876, and the effects of the so-called Compromise of 1877 on the South and on the nation.

10. The methods used by white Southerners to regain control of the region's politics.

11. The reasons for the failure of the South to develop a strong industrial economy after Reconstruction.

12. The ways in which Southerners decided to handle the race question, and the origin of the system identified with "Jim Crow."

13.   The response of blacks to conditions in the South following Reconstruction.

PERTINENT QUESTIONS

The Problems of Peacemaking (pp. 442–449)

1.   What effects did the Civil War have on the economy and social system of the South?

2.   What special problems did the freedmen face immediately after the war? What efforts were made to help them?

3.   What political implications did the readmission of the Southern states pose for the political parties, especially the Republicans?

4.   What were the differences among the Conservative, Radical, and Moderate factions of the Republican Party during Reconstruction?

5.   What were the objectives and provisions of Lincoln's plan for Reconstruction? How did the Radical Republicans respond to it?

6.   Describe Andrew Johnson's approach to Reconstruction. How was it shaped by his political background and his personality?

Radical Reconstruction (pp. 449–455)

7.   Describe the Black Codes and the congressional reaction to them. How did President Johnson respond to Congress?

8.   What were the key provisions of the Fourteenth Amendment? What happened to it in 1866?

9.   Explain the basic provisions of the congressional plan of Reconstruction of 1867 and tell how it was implemented. What were the implications of waiting so long after the war to get a comprehensive plan in place?

10.   What measures did the Radical Republicans take to keep President Johnson and the Supreme Court from interfering with their plans? What ultimately happened to Johnson's influence?

The South in Reconstruction (pp. 455–461)

11.   What three groups constituted the Republican Party in the South during Reconstruction?

12.   How do the facts of political life in the Reconstruction states compare to the oft-stated white charges of corruption, black domination, and misrule?

13.   What changes in Southern education began to emerge during Reconstruction? Who pushed for these changes?

14. What changes in land ownership occurred in the South after the Civil War? What pattern of land occupancy characterized most blacks in the postwar South?

15. How did the typical agricultural credit system in the postwar South affect farmers—especially poor ones?

16. What economic advances did the freedmen make? How did the economic status of blacks compare with that of the average white Southerner?

17. How did freedom affect black family life?

The Grant Administration (pp. 462–464)

18. How did Ulysses S. Grant's political accomplishments compare with his military ability?

19. What episodes led to the Liberal Republican break over "Grantism" and later to the second-term scandals?

20. People in what financial condition were most likely to favor expansion of the currency supply with greenbacks? What sparked interest in greenbacks?

The Abandonment of Reconstruction (pp. 465–469)

21. What tactics did *white* Southern Democrats use to restrict or control black suffrage?

22. Why did Northern Republicans begin to take less interest in Reconstruction and the cause of the freedmen after about 1870?

23. Why was the presidential election of 1876 disputed? How was the controversy resolved by the "Compromise of 1877"?

24. What was President Rutherford B. Hayes's objective in the South? Did he succeed?

25. Compare white and black expectations for Reconstruction with the actual results. Why were most black hopes dashed? What black gains were made?

The New South (pp. 469–477)

26. What were the typical socioeconomic and political characteristics of the "Redeemers" (Bourbons)?

27. How did the policies of the "Redeemer" governments compare with those of the Reconstruction-era administrations?

28. In what particular products was industrialization in the South most advanced? What factors attracted industrial capital to the region after the war?

29. Describe the composition of the industrial work force in the South. What was life in a mill town like?

30. Describe the typical pattern of Southern agriculture in the late nineteenth and early twentieth centuries. What problems confronted most farmers? What groups were most notably affected?
31. Describe the rise of the black middle class.
32. What was Booker T. Washington's prescription for black advancement as expressed in the "Atlanta Compromise" and elsewhere?
33. How did the civil rights cases of 1883 and *Plessy* v. *Ferguson* (1896) substantially negate the effect of the equal-protection clause of the Fourteenth Amendment?
34. What strategies and legal devices did the Southern states use to evade the spirit of the Fifteenth Amendment? What motivated the late-nineteenth–early-twentieth century crackdown on black voting?
35. Describe the pervasive nature of "Jim Crow" laws. How was the system enforced, formally and informally?
36. Explain the historic debate over Reconstruction and show how the various interpretations were reflections of the time in which they were written.

IDENTIFICATION

Identify each of the following, and explain why it is important within the context of the chapter.
1. Lincoln's plan for Reconstruction
2. O. O. Howard
3. Thaddeus Stevens
4. Charles Sumner
5. Wade-Davis Bill
6. John Wilkes Booth
7. Alexander H. Stephens
8. Joint Committee on Reconstruction
9. Edwin M. Stanton
10. scalawag
11. carpetbagger
12. sharecropping
13. spoils system/civil service
14. Crédit Mobilier
15. "whiskey ring"
16. Hamilton Fish
17. "Seward's Folly"

18. *"Alabama"* claims
19. "redeemed"
20. Ku Klux Klan
21. Samuel J. Tilden
22. "solid" Democratic South
23. Henry W. Grady
24. lynching

DOCUMENT

Read the portions of the chapter that discuss the Black Codes. Also read the "Debating the Past" discussion (p. 450). The following selection is taken from the writings of William A. Dunning. Consider the following questions: How does Dunning's account reveal his racist assumptions? How would accounts such as Dunning's lead white southerners in the twentieth century to conclude that they had been gravely wronged by Reconstruction? Which of the following statements is more convincing: The Black Codes were a necessary and realistic response to the situation. The Black Codes were a thinly disguised attempt to resubjugate the freedmen.

> To a distrustful northern mind such legislation could very easily take the form of a systematic attempt to relegate the freedmen to a subjection only less complete than that from which the war had set them free. The radicals sounded a shrill note of alarm. "We tell the white men of Mississippi," said the Chicago *Tribune,* "that the men of the North will convert the state of Mississippi into a frog-pond before they will allow any such laws to disgrace one foot of soil over which the flag of freedom waves." In Congress, Wilson, Sumner, and other extremists took up the cry, and with superfluous ingenuity distorted the spirit and purpose of both the laws and the law-makers of the South. The "black codes" were represented to be the expression of a deliberate purpose by the southerners to nullify the result of the war and reestablish slavery, and this impression gained wide prevalence in the North.
>
> Yet, as a matter of fact, this legislation, far from embodying any spirit of defiance towards the North or any purpose to evade the conditions which the victors had imposed, was in the main a conscientious and straightforward attempt to bring some sort of order out of the social and economic chaos which a full acceptance of the results of war and emancipation involved. In its general principle it corresponded very closely to the actual facts of the situation. The freedmen were not, and in the nature of the case could not for generations be, on the same social, moral, and intellectual plane with the whites; and this fact was recognized by constituting them a separate class in the civil order. As in general principles, so in details, the legislation was faithful on the whole to the actual conditions with which it had to deal. The restrictions in respect to bearing arms, testifying in court, and keeping labor contracts were justified by well-established traits and habits of the negroes; and the vagrancy laws dealt with problems of destitution, idleness, and vice of which no one not in the midst of them could appreciate the appalling magnitude and complexity.

William A. Dunning, *Reconstruction: Political and Economic, 1865–1877* (1907; reprint, New York: Harper & Row [Harper Torchbooks], 1962), pp. 57–58.

MAP EXERCISE

Fill in or identify the following on the blank map provided.

1. Former Confederate states.
2. First state to be readmitted, including the year.
3. Last three states to be readmitted, including the years. (Note that the other seven were readmitted in 1868.)
4. First three states to reestablish Conservative government, including the years.
5. States in which Conservative government was not reestablished until 1876.

Interpretative Questions

Based on what you have filled in, answer the following. For some of the questions you will need to consult the narrative in your text for information or explanation.

1. Note the location of the first state to be readmitted by Congress, and explain why it was restored to the Union so quickly.
2. What did the other ten states have to do to gain their readmissions in 1868–1870?

3. Note the first three states to experience the reestablishment of Conservative government and explain why the restoration of Democratic Party rule came so quickly there.
4. What forces delayed the reestablishment of the Conservative government in the other states? What episode symbolically marks the end of the Reconstruction era?

SUMMARY

The military aspect of the American Civil War lasted less than five years and ended in April 1865, but it would take another dozen years of Reconstruction to determine what the results of the war would be. The only questions clearly settled by the time of Appomattox were that the nation was indivisible and that slavery must end. The nation faced other issues with far-reaching implications. What would be the place of the freedmen in Southern society? How would the rebellious states be brought back into their "proper relationship" with the Union? The victorious North was in a position to dominate the South, but Northern politicians were not united in either resolve or purpose. For over two years after the fighting stopped, there was no coherent Reconstruction policy. Congress and the president struggled with each other, and various factions in Congress had differing views on politics, race, and union. Congress finally won control and dominated the Reconstruction process until Southern resistance and Northern ambivalence led to the end of Reconstruction in 1877. In the years that followed, a "New South" emerged, whose leaders believed the region could be modernized through industrial development. But despite their efforts the South's agricultural sector remained predominant. No economic, political, or social issue in the South could escape the race question. The Jim Crow system created by white Southerners succeeded in evading the spirit of the Fourteenth and Fifteenth Amendments, and black hopes for political equality faded. Although enormous changes had taken place, the era left a legacy of continuing racism and sectionalism.

CHAPTER SELF-TEST

After you have read the chapter in the text and done the exercises in the study guide, the following self-test can be taken to see if you understand the material you have covered. Answers appear at the end of the study guide.

Multiple Choice

Circle the letter of the response that best answers the question or completes the statement.

1. The Thirteenth Amendment to the U.S. Constitution:
    a. declared that the right to vote could not be denied on account of race.
    b. officially ended slavery.
    c. granted "citizenship" to the freedmen.
    d. provided that states could only count three-fifths (60 percent) of their black population when determining how many members they would be given in the U.S. House of Representatives.
    e. opened up the West to homesteading by African Americans.

2. The Fourteenth Amendment to the U.S. Constitution:
    a. declared that the right to vote could not be denied on account of race.
    b. officially ended slavery.
    c. granted "citizenship" to the freedmen.
    d. provided that states could only count three-fifths (60 percent) of their black population when determining how many members they would be given in the U.S. House of Representatives.
    e. opened up the West to homesteading by African Americans.

3. The Fifteenth Amendment to the U.S. Constitution:
    a. declared that the right to vote could not be denied on account of race.
    b. officially ended slavery.
    c. granted "citizenship" to the freedmen.
    d. provided that states could only count three-fifths (60 percent) of their black population when determining how many members they would be given in the U.S. House of Representatives.
    e. opened up the West to homesteading by African Americans.

4. Which faction of the Republican Party wanted Reconstruction to punish the former Confederacy, disfranchise large numbers of Southern whites, and confiscate the property of leading Confederates?
    a. Moderates
    b. Conservatives
    c. Redeemers
    d. Scalywaggers
    e. Radicals

5. Which best describes Congressional reaction to the former Confederate states that had set up new governments under Andrew Johnson's "presidential Reconstruction"?
   a. They fully accepted all of the states except Georgia and South Carolina, which had elected no blacks to office.
   b. They conditionally accepted all of the states pending the results of local and state elections.
   c. They refused to seat the senators and representatives from the states and set up a committee to investigate and advise on Reconstruction.
   d. They fully accepted all of the states west of the Mississippi River, but required new constitutions in the others.

6. The "Black Codes" were a set of regulations established by:
   a. Congress to protect the rights of the former slaves to own property and to find employment.
   b. the U.S. Supreme Court to enforce the provisions of the Thirteenth and Fourteenth Amendments to the U.S. Constitution.
   c. the Northern states to prevent a massive influx of former slaves from entering their states and seeking homes and jobs.
   d. the Southern states to promote white supremacy and to control the economic and social activities of the freedmen.

7. Which of the following, if any, was *not* a provision of the congressional plan of Reconstruction enacted in early 1867?
   a. Dividing the South into military districts administered by military commanders
   b. Requiring former Confederate states, as a condition of readmission to the Union, to ratify the Fourteenth Amendment to the U.S. Constitution
   c. Mandating former Confederate states, as a condition of readmission to the union, to hold a constitutional convention and prepare a constitution providing for black male suffrage
   d. Declaring that each state must present a plan for distributing farmland to or providing jobs for the former slaves
   e. All of the above were provisions of the congressional plan of Reconstruction

8. Critics of native Southern whites who joined the Republican Party called them:
   a. carpetbaggers.
   b. whippersnappers.
   c. scalawags.
   d. white camellias.
   e. filibusterers.

9. Which best describes the extent of "Negro rule" in the Southern states during Reconstruction?
   a. African Americans played a significant political role in several states but never elected a governor or controlled a state legislature.
   b. Some African Americans held local elective offices and a very few were elected to state legislatures but the numbers were politically inconsequential in every state.
   c. In the Deep South states where African Americans constituted a majority of the voters due to white disfranchisement, blacks dominated both houses of the state legislatures and controlled state politics as long as federal troops remained in the South.
   d. African Americans did not actually hold many offices in any state, but they effectively dominated local offices in all but Tennessee and Arkansas through alliances with white Republicans.

10. The key point of contact in the agricultural credit system for most Southern farmers, black and white, in the late nineteenth century was:
    a. small-town banks owned by Northerners.
    b. large diversified planters.
    c. finance companies in the larger cities such as Atlanta and Memphis.
    d. local country store merchants.
    e. mail-order mortgage companies operating out of New York.

11. In the late nineteenth century, the agricultural credit system in the South encouraged farmers to:
    a. rely heavily on cash crops—especially cotton.
    b. diversify away from cotton toward food grains and livestock.
    c. adopt the use of mechanization on increasingly larger farms.
    d. abandon farming and invest in capital-intensive manufacturing enterprises.

12. Ulysses S. Grant's election as president was largely a result of his being:
    a. governor of New York during the postwar economic boom.
    b. a triumphant commanding general of the Union army.
    c. the popular administrator of the Freedmen's Bureau.
    d. a flamboyant cavalry officer in the western Indian wars.

13. Which of the following, if any, was *not* associated with the "Compromise of 1877"?
    a. Removal of the last federal troops from the South
    b. Increased federal aid for railroads and other internal improvements
    c. Appointment of a Southerner to the cabinet
    d. Making Rutherford B. Hayes president
    e. All of the above are associated with the "Compromise of 1877."

14. Which of the following, if any, is *not* cited by the text as a reason that Reconstruction failed to accomplish more to promote racial equality in the United States?
    a. Fear that harsh action might lead to resumed military action by the Southern states, even though they had been defeated
    b. Attachment to a states' rights view of the Constitution, even for the rebel states
    c. Deep respect for private property rights, even for leading Confederates
    d. Belief in black inferiority by many whites, even Northern liberals
    e. All of the above were cited as reasons that Reconstruction failed to accomplish more.

15. The "solid" South refers to the:
    a. work ethic values of Southern whites.
    b. courage of Confederate soldiers during the war despite being outnumbered.
    c. steady returns that Northern bankers could expect from investment in cotton.
    d. fact that the Democratic Party could count on the votes of the Southern states after Reconstruction.

16. In most Southern states, the "Redeemers" or "Bourbons" were typically composed of:
    a. a newly emerging class of merchants, industrialists, railroad developers, and financiers.
    b. essentially the same old planter elite that had dominated antebellum politics.
    c. a coalition of poor, working-class whites and blacks.
    d. white farmers who owned small to medium farms.

17. Henry W. Grady was:
    a. the builder of the American Tobacco Company.
    b. an Atlanta editor who became a leading spokesman for the "New South" idea.
    c. the person principally responsible for Birmingham, Alabama, becoming an iron and steel production center.
    d. the governor of South Carolina who was most vociferous in advocating that blacks should migrate from the South to take industrial jobs in the North.

18. Booker T. Washington's principal message to African Americans was that they should:
    a. concentrate on practical, industrial education and work toward adopting the standards of the white middle class.
    b. join in common economic interests with white workers to bring the trade union movement to the South so that the wages would rise for all.
    c. strive first for full voting rights because only political power could bring economic gain.
    d. abandon the South and seek factory jobs in the North where segregation was less of a problem.

19. "Jim Crow" is a nickname for:
    a. white Southerners who used violence or intimidation to restrict black activities.
    b. black people who curried favor with whites by acting excessively polite and deferential.
    c. the whole system of laws and customs that kept the races separate in schools, public buildings, housing, jobs, theaters, etc.
    d. black people who pretended to be friendly toward whites but who secretly undermined white interests.
    e. the African-American culture of dance, music, food, and religion that grew up after slavery.

20. In *Plessy* v. *Ferguson* (1896) the U.S. Supreme Court established the general principle that:
   a. states could not prevent blacks from voting just because their grandparents had been slaves.
   b. states could require separate accommodations on trains, in schools, etc., for blacks and whites as long as the accommodations were equal.
   c. Congress could take away a state's seats in the U.S. House of Representatives if the state refused to allow blacks to vote in congressional elections.
   d. local governments could use zoning and building codes to enforce racial segregation by neighborhood.

True/False

Read each statement carefully. Mark true statements "T" and false statements "F."

___1.   As bad as the economic and physical situation was for Southern blacks in the aftermath of the Civil War, conditions were even worse for the region's white population.

___2.   The Emancipation Proclamation ended slavery throughout the South in 1863.

___3.   Republicans were afraid that the quick return of the Southern states to Congress would lead to more Democratic votes, thereby increasing the likelihood that Congress would establish protective tariffs and subsidize railroads.

___4.   President Lincoln believed that a lenient Reconstruction policy would encourage Southern Unionists and other Southern Whigs to become Republicans and build a stronger party in the South.

___5.   John Wilkes Booth acted completely on his own in plotting to murder President Lincoln.

___6.   Characteristics of Andrew Johnson's personality that hampered him as president were that he was too polite and deferential to assume any leadership initiative.

___7.   The Tenure of Office Act and the Command of the Army Act were passed by Congress to prevent Southern states from sending former Confederates to Congress or from having them control the state militia companies.

___8.   Even though the House's impeachment charges were nominally based on specific "high crimes and misdemeanors," Andrew Johnson was actually convicted by the Senate and removed from the presidency for petty political reasons.

___9. Despite the end of slavery, most black agricultural labor in the South in the late nineteenth century continued to emulate the gang-labor system in which slaves lived in concentrated quarters and worked in groups under the constant supervision of a white field boss suggestive of the prewar overseer.

___10. During the period from just before the Civil War to just after Reconstruction, per capita income for African Americans rose significantly while per capita income for whites dropped.

___11. In the 1870s, the expanded printing of greenback paper currency was advocated by those, especially debtors, who believed that inflation would help the economy.

___12. In the context of Reconstruction, "redeemed" was used to refer to freedmen who had returned to their original slave plantations as workers after running away during or immediately following the war.

___13. The Crédit Mobilier was a railroad construction company involved in scandal during the Grant administration.

___14. Hamilton Fish was Grant's secretary of state whose action worsened relations between the United States and Great Britain.

___15. Alaska was called "Seward's Folly" because of his abortive attempt to sell the territory to the Russian czar as a method of financing the cost of maintaining troops in the South during Reconstruction.

___16. In the period from the end of Reconstruction into the twentieth century, the Democratic Party was the political party of the vast majority of Southern whites.

___17. In general, the "Redeemer" ("Bourbon") political regimes were inclined to raise taxes to expand services, especially public education.

___18. By 1900 the portion of the nation's manufacturing output produced in the South was about three times what it had been on the eve of the Civil War.

___19. The portion of Southern farmers who were tenants, cash or sharecrop, increased markedly from Reconstruction to 1900.

___20. In the period from Reconstruction to 1900, the crop-lien system helped force many Southern backcountry farmers in the piney woods and mountains from cash crop commercial farming into a ruggedly independent sort of subsistence farming.

___21. By the late 1890s, a significantly smaller portion of Southern blacks was allowed to vote than in the late 1860s.

Review Questions

These questions are to be answered with essays. This will allow you to explore relationships among individuals, events, and attitudes of the period under review.

1. Compare and contrast the several plans for Reconstruction: Lincoln's plan, the Wade-Davis Bill, Johnson's presidential Reconstruction, and the congressional plan. Consider provisions, motives, goals, and results. What forces and attitudes kept a more radical plan from being adopted?

2. Evaluate the successes and failures of Reconstruction. Given the context of the times, explain what, if anything, could have been done to avoid the failures and expand the successes. What groundwork was laid for the future?

3. Although many changes had occurred by 1900, the South remained an impoverished agricultural region, lagging well behind the rest of the nation. Describe the economic changes in the South, and assess why they were not adequate to bring the old Confederacy into the national mainstream, as some of the region's spokespersons had hoped.

4. Explain the ways in which the Southern white establishment was able to evade the spirit of the Fourteenth and Fifteenth Amendments to the Constitution. What alternative paths of accommodation and resistance did black leaders propose to this rise of Jim Crow?

CHAPTER SIXTEEN

The Conquest of the Far West

OBJECTIVES

A thorough study of Chapter 16 should enable you to understand:

1. The cultural characteristics of the varied populations of the Far West and the conflicts among them.
2. The ways that the western economy evolved toward modern capitalism in terms of mining, cattle raising, and commercial farming.
3. How white culture and federal policy worked to destroy Indian culture in the West.
4. The process by which the West opened to commercial farming and the problems that the farmers faced.

PERTINENT QUESTIONS

The Societies of the Far West (pp. 481–490)

1. Compare and contrast the Pacific Coast Indians with the Pueblos of the Southwest.
2. What traits did the Plains tribes share, and what was the economic basis of the way of life for most Plains tribes?
3. What were the key disadvantages that the Plains Indians had in their conflicts with white settlers?
4. How did Anglo-American dominance affect the nature of Indian and Hispanic culture in New Mexico from the 1840s to 1900?
5. What factors led to the decline of Mexican-American economic and social dominance in California and Texas? What was the socioeconomic status of most Mexican Americans by the end of the nineteenth century?
6. In what fields did most Chinese immigrants work? How did employment, residential patterns, and social relations in the Chinese-American community change as the century progressed?

7. What led to the increasing Anglo-European hostility toward the Chinese in California? What were the social and public policy results of this hostility?
8. What led to the late-nineteenth-century boom in migration to the West from the eastern United States and Europe?
9. How did the federal government assist settlers in obtaining western land through the Homestead Act and other laws?
10. Given the rapid political progression from territory to state in most of the West, why did Utah, Arizona, New Mexico, and Oklahoma lag behind?

The Changing Western Economy (pp. 490–496)

11. What was the composition and structure of the labor force in the West? How was it shaped by racial prejudice?
12. What were the principal gold and silver boom areas from 1859 to 1874?
13. Describe the typical pattern of development and decline in the mining regions. What was life like for men and women in the mining camps and towns?
14. Describe the origins, purposes, and practices of the "long drive" and the "open range" cattle industry. What ended this brief but colorful boom?
15. What opportunities opened to women in the West that were not available in the East?

The Romance of the West (pp. 496–499)

16. How did the Wild West shows of Buffalo Bill Cody and others shape the popular image of the American West?
17. What did Frederick Jackson Turner conclude about the importance of the western frontier? According to the "Debating the Past" selection of p. 500 how influential was his thesis? How did the "new western historians" and others challenge the Turner view?

The Dispersal of the Tribes (pp. 499–508)

18. Describe the evolution of basic national Indian policy up to the 1880s. How successful was it for whites? For the Indians?
19. What happened to the great buffalo herds? How was Plains Indian life affected?

20. Describe the general pattern of Indian wars from the 1850s to the 1880s. What were the largest and most violent conflicts? Why did whites ultimately prevail? What did white tactics in subduing the tribes indicate about the dominant culture's attitude toward women?

21. What actions were taken under the Dawes Act, and what basic objective did the federal government hope to achieve by this legislation?

The Rise and Decline of the Western Farmer (pp. 508–513)

22. Describe the building and financing of the transcontinental railroads. What was the impact on the West?

23. What problems not typical of the East did farmers encounter on the Great Plains? What methods and devices helped solve these problems? What problems remained?

24. How were market forces changing the nature of American agriculture in this period? What was the result?

25. What were the three main grievances of the late-nineteenth-century farmer? How were these complaints compounded by attitudinal factors?

IDENTIFICATION

Identify each of the following, and explain why it is important within the context of the chapter.

1. *californios*
2. "coolies"
3. Chinatown
4. "tongs"
5. "range wars"
6. "Rocky Mountain School," Albert Bierstadt, and Thomas Moran
7. *The Virginian*
8. Frederic Remington
9. Indian Territory (Oklahoma)
10. Indian Peace Commission
11. Bureau of Indian Affairs
12. Sand Creek episode
13. Crazy Horse and Sitting Bull
14. George A. Custer
15. Nez Percé
16. Geronimo
17. Wounded Knee incident

DOCUMENT

An editorial in the Atlanta *Constitution,* one of the leading newspapers of the postwar South, heralded the completion of the transcontinental railroad in 1896. In light of this and the previous chapter, consider the following questions: How does the editorial reveal the psychological importance of the transcontinental railroad to the American sense of nationhood? How does it show that the railroad would lead to the closing of the Far West frontier? What does the writer reveal about southern jealousy of sorthern industrial accomplishment?

This mammoth enterprise is completed at last. It has no equal in modern history for magnitude, importance, and the energy of its execution. Bold in conception and stupendous in realization, it stands a monument among the monster achievements of the age. It links the oceans with its iron bond. It brings the continents into close social and commercial communion. It nullifies the area of immense distances and overlaps the impediments of boundless wilderness. It pierces savage realms with the probe of civilization. It hitches progress on to the barren domination of the uncultured Indian. It connects the buffalo with the water-fall. With the speed of lightning it transmits the refinements of high polish and the improvements of progressive art and science broadcast over a country that must have remained otherwise a free range of wild forest. It redeems from disuse millions of acres of virgin land, and is the "opening up" [of] a stream of commerce and development that will beneficially inundate one of the magnificent portions of the world.

It is useless to dispute the wonderful spirit of energy and skill that has put this herculean enterprise through. The difficulties have been almost invincible, and the nerve to overcome them has been grand.

But this success has some grave drawbacks concerned with it. . . . It might have been built elsewhere with less money and served the purposes of its construction better. . . . The Southern Pacific route is destined to be the successful road between the two oceans. It is shorter than the one now built, runs through a milder climate, has less obstacles of mountain and river, and can be used all the year round. . . . We regard the Southern Pacific as one of the necessities of Southern effort. It will do more to build up our Southern states than any other one business movement. When we get to be the channel for the stupendous tide of commerce and trade that will surge over the land from the Pacific coast, we will spring into potent importance, and we will absorb and assimilate unreckonable wealth and population. Let us grasp for the huge prize. Let us no longer sit confessed sluggards in contrast with Northern energy. Let us not sit supinely and see our Northern neighbor pick fruits that belong to us legitimately.

Constitution, 12 May 1869, p. 1.

MAP EXERCISE

Fill in or identify the following on the blank map provided.

1. Draw a line indicating the western rim of English-speaking settlement as of 1860. Circle the pockets of such settlement in the Far West.
2. Indicate the area of the Great Plains by means of diagonal lines.
3. Draw lines indicating the general flow of the "long drives."
4. Indicate the Rocky Mountains and the Sierra Nevada–Cascade Range by drawing inverted *V*s along their positions.
5. Place boxes with dates to indicate the general areas of the gold and silver rushes of 1849, 1858 to 1859, and 1874. Tell what state each strike was in.
6. Draw a line along the route of the first transcontinental railroad. Place a star at the point where the two lines joined. Also draw the routes of subsequent transcontinental railroads.
7. Identify Indian Territory (Oklahoma) with "I.T." and the Dakotas with "N.D." and "S.D."

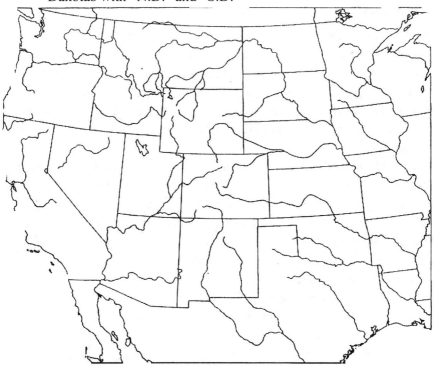

Interpretative Questions

Based on what you have filled in, answer the following. For some of the questions you will need to consult the narrative in your text for information or explanation.

1. Why did the frontier line stop where it did around 1860?
2. How was the pre–Civil War settlement along the Pacific Coast isolated from the rest of the nation?
3. Why did the post–Civil War gold and silver rushes involve considerable west-to-east as well as east-to-west migration?
4. What long-term effects did the "cattle kingdom" boom have?
5. Why were the Plains Indians so resentful of the reservations they were provided?
6. What areas of the nation were best served by the first transcontinental railroad? Why was the South resentful?
7. What special challenges did agriculture on the Great Plains present to farmers?

SUMMARY

Far from being empty and unknown, significant parts of what would become the western United States were populated by Indians and Hispanics long before the post–Civil War boom in eastern and European settlement. Even after the waves of white occupation and in the face of significant prejudice from those whites, large numbers of Mexican and Asian Americans continued to live in the West and influence its culture and economy.

White settlement developed in initial boom-and-decline patterns in the three industries that would do much to shape the region in the long run: mining, ranching, and commercial agriculture. Asians, Mexicans, and, to a lesser extent, African Americans provided much of the labor force for these endeavors.

In much of the West, and especially in the plains and the Southwest, hostile Indians violently resisted white encroachment because it threatened to destroy their culture. Due to better organization and equipment and the force of numbers, whites prevailed in battle and implemented policies designed to destroy tribal identity. Even with the increased access by rail and improved farming techniques, agriculture on the Great Plains was a challenge. Frustrated farmers had more grievances than solutions.

CHAPTER SELF-TEST

After you have read the chapter in the text and done the exercises in the study guide, the following self-test can be taken to see if you understand the material you have covered. Answers appear at the end of the study guide.

Multiple Choice

Circle the letter of the response that best answers the question or completes the statement.

1. Because the area was arid to semiarid and thought to be unfit for Anglo-European civilization, many early-nineteenth-century Americans called the Far West the:
    a. Trans-Mississippi Wasteland.
    b. Intermountain Barrens.
    c. Prairie Wilderness.
    d. Great American Desert.

2. Indian Territory, to which several eastern Indian tribes, including the Cherokees and the Creeks, were removed, is now the state of:
    a. Nebraska.
    b. Kansas.
    c. Oklahoma.
    d. Wyoming.

3. What happened to the *californios* who dominated California prior to the gold rush of 1849?
    a. Most died due to epidemic diseases brought in by the miners.
    b. The ones who could speak English adapted well and continued to dominate real estate ownership.
    c. Most emigrated back to Mexico or Arizona.
    d. They lost status and land and were excluded from Anglo-dominated prosperity.

4. Up to 1869, the great majority of Chinese Americans worked in what *two* industries? (Choose two letters.)
    a. Mining (especially gold)
    b. Services (domestic work, laundry, etc.)
    c. Railroads (especially construction)
    d. Retailing (small merchants)

5. Which of the following was *not* a reason for Anglo-American resentment of Chinese immigrants?
   a. They tended to congregate together and maintain Chinese culture.
   b. Some secret societies ("tongs") engaged in crime.
   c. Many of the early female Chinese immigrants had been sold into prostitution.
   d. The Chinese were perceived as lazy slackers who would not work hard.

6. Which of the following was the main flaw in the Homestead Act?
   a. 160 acres was not enough land for grazing and grain farming in the West.
   b. African Americans were prohibited from obtaining land under the act.
   c. The fees involved in establishing ownership of land were too costly for most settlers.

7. Which of the following was *not* a state by 1900?
   a. Colorado
   b. California
   c. Nevada
   d. Oklahoma

8. Which type of mining came first as new fields opened?
   a. Placer (surface)
   b. Quartz (lode)
   c. Open pit (blasting)

9. Which of the following states and/or territories did *not* experience significant mining development from the 1850s to the 1880s?
   a. Nevada
   b. Colorado
   c. Kansas
   d. South Dakota
   e. Montana

10. The "long drive" in the open-range cattle industry referred to the process of:
    a. rounding up the cattle from great distances all over the range in the spring for branding.
    b. moving the cattle south to Texas in the winter and north to Colorado, Wyoming, and Montana in the spring to take advantage of the best pastures.

c. using cattle as oxen to pull covered wagons for settlers seeking homesteads in the West.

d. herding cattle from the ranges in Texas and other remote areas to the nearest accessible railroad loading point so that the cattle could be shipped to slaughterhouses in the East.

11. The so-called range wars of the West were between (choose two letters):
   a. white and black cowboys.
   b. sheep ranchers and cattle ranchers.
   c. Hispanics and Anglo landowners.
   d. farmers and ranchers.

12. The federal government agency vested with management of Indian relations and the reservations was the:
   a. Indian Lands Commission.
   b. Native American Administration.
   c. Office of Assimilation and Concentration.
   d. Bureau of Indian Affairs.

13. The two principal Indian chiefs who led the forces that massed in the northern plains in 1875–1876 following the Black Hills gold rush were (choose two letters):
   a. Black Kettle.
   b. Sitting Bull.
   c. Crazy Horse.
   d. Geronimo.
   e. Red Eagle.

14. The purpose of the Dawes Severalty Act of 1887 was to:
   a. weaken tribes, allot land to individual Indians, and promote assimilation.
   b. geographically disperse the reservations so it would be more difficult for Indian warrior forces to unite.
   c. increase tribal loyalty and reduce violence by allowing chiefs and tribal councils to act autonomously on the reservations.
   d. restore economic viability to the nomadic way of Plains Indian life by revitalizing the bison herds.

15. Which of the following was *not* a way that farmers adapted to life on the Great Plains up through the 1890s?
   a. Barbed wire fencing
   b. Drought-resistant crops and farming methods
   c. Large-scale government-funded irrigation
   d. Deep wells with windmill-driven pumps

True/False

Read each statement carefully. Mark true statements "T" and false statements "F."

___1.   As late as 1900, the Far West remained essentially outside America's capitalist economy.

___2.   The Indians of the plains and Pacific Coast proved to be remarkably resistant to the diseases that afflicted Anglo-European settlers.

___3.   Although most historians have previously treated the buffalo as critical to Plains Indian culture prior to the 1880s, recent anthropological work has revealed that this is a myth and that the buffalo was actually relatively unimportant for these tribes.

___4.   Prior to the arrival of significant numbers of English-speaking settlers, an elite of landowning Hispanics dominated life in California.

___5.   The "Rocky Mountain School" of artists mostly painted realistic pictures that showed the rigorous lives of trappers, miners, and cowboys.

___6.   "Coolies" were Chinese indentured servants whose status was close to slavery.

___7.   In the late nineteenth century, most California residents favored increased Chinese immigration because there was a labor shortage and the Chinese would work for low wages.

___8.   The Timber Culture Act, Desert Land Act, and Timber and Stone Act provided avenues for westerners to acquire larger tracts of land than were allowed under the Homestead Act.

___9.   The working class in the American West was racially diversified and stratified.

___10.   The so-called Turner thesis argued that the existence of the frontier was vitally important to the shaping of the American character.

___11.   Prostitution was common in the mining boomtowns.

___12.   When the "long drive" era began, there was an excess of cattle in Texas, so cowboys drove huge herds to rail centers in Louisiana, especially New Orleans, for shipment to the East.

___13.   Although the Bureau of Indian Affairs was chronically underfunded and understaffed, the reform-minded whites who ran it established a solid reputation for honesty, efficiency, and sincere concern for the well-being of the Native Americans they served.

___14. Although small, the Nez Percé tribe was composed of particularly effective warriors who engaged in raids throughout the southern plains until Chief Joseph was finally captured in 1877.

___15. The first transcontinental railroad was completed shortly before the beginning of the Civil War, but due to wartime disruption it did not carry much traffic until the end of the 1860s.

Review Questions

These questions are to be answered with essays. This will allow you to explore relationships among individuals, events, and attitudes of the period under review.

1. Explain how the mining, cattle, and farming frontiers followed something of a boom-and-bust pattern. Evaluate the long-term impact of the frontier activities on the development of the West.

2. What was the role of women in the far western mining and railroad towns and on ranches and farms? How did the role change with time?

3. How did white racial, ethnic, and cultural prejudice against Indians, Mexicans, and Asians shape the development of the American West?

4. Compare and contrast the regional socioeconomic characteristics of the post–Civil War South and West.

CHAPTER SEVENTEEN

Industrial Supremacy

OBJECTIVES

A thorough study of Chapter 17 should enable you to understand:

1. The reasons for the rapid industrial development of the United States in the late nineteenth century.
2. The specific impact of technological innovation in promoting industrial expansion.
3. The role of the individual entrepreneur in the development of particular industries.
4. The changes that were taking place in American business organization.
5. The ways in which classical economics and certain ideas of Darwin were used to justify and defend the new industrial capitalism.
6. The critics of the new industrial capitalism and the solutions they proposed.
7. The condition of immigrants, women, and children in the work force.
8. The rise of organized labor on a national federated basis.
9. The reasons why organized labor generally failed in its efforts to achieve its objectives.

PERTINENT QUESTIONS

Sources of Industrial Growth (pp. 516–527)

1. How did the late-nineteenth-century technological innovations in communications and office productivity impact the conduct of business?
2. What impact did the increasingly widespread use of electricity as a source of light and power have on homes and industry?

3. What new technologies were developed for the large-scale production of durable steel? What impact did the vast expansion of steel production have on transportation industries in the late nineteenth century?
4. Describe the beginnings of the oil industry in the United States. What was the main use of petroleum at first?
5. Although the age of the automobile and the era of significant American aircraft production would not fully arrive until the 1910s and 1920s, what developments of the 1890s and the first decade of the twentieth century laid the basis for the later boom?
6. How did expanding research and development activities and "scientific management" reshape American industrial production? What role did the Ford Motor Company play in these early-twentieth-century developments?
7. How did the rapidly expanding railroads of this era contribute to the expansion of the American economy?
8. Describe how the railroads took the lead in new patterns of business organization and management in the late nineteenth century. What legal and financial advantages does the corporation form of enterprise offer to business and investors?
9. Compare and contrast the vertical and horizontal integration strategies of business combination. Which approaches did Andrew Carnegie and John D. Rockefeller utilize? What "curse" of the business world was consolidation designed to attack?
10. What were the consequences of the consolidation movement?

Capitalism and Its Critics (pp. 527–533)

11. What kept alive the "self-made man" hopes of the American masses? How realistic were such "Horatio Alger stories"?
12. What was the theory of Social Darwinism and how did it seem to justify the acquisition of great wealth?
13. Who were the leading proponents of vigorous governmental action to reform industrial society? What visions did they have?
14. What inspired the increasing resentment of monopoly by many groups?

The Ordeal of the Worker (pp. 533–543)

15. America's new urban working class was drawn primarily from what two groups?
16. Contrast the earlier immigrants to the United States with those who came after the 1880s. What attracted immigrants to the United States?

17. What were the uncertainties and hazards of industrial labor?
18. Why did industry increasingly employ women and children? How were they treated?
19. What was America's first major labor conflict and how did it end? What new economic reality did its scale illustrate?
20. Compare and contrast the organization, membership, leadership, and programs of the Knights of Labor and the American Federation of Labor. Why did the AFL succeed, while the Knights disappeared?
21. Compare and contrast the Haymarket affair, Homestead strike, and Pullman strike. On balance, what was their effect on the organized labor movement?
22. What factors combined to help explain why organized labor remained relatively weak before World War I?

IDENTIFICATION

Identify each of the following, and explain why it is important within the context of the chapter.
1. Alexander Graham Bell
2. Thomas A. Edison
3. Guglielmo Marconi
4. Orville Wright and Wilbur Wright
5. Charles Duryea and Frank Duryea
6. Frederick Winslow Taylor
7. Cornelius Vanderbilt
8. J. P. Morgan
9. Isaac Singer
10. "middle manager"
11. pool (cartel)
12. trust
13. holding company
14. Herbert Spencer
15. William Graham Sumner
16. "gospel of wealth"
17. Horatio Alger
18. Daniel DeLeon
19. Socialist Labor Party
20. Henry George
21. Edward Bellamy
22. the Molly Maguires

23. Samuel Gompers
24. anarchism
25. Eugene V. Debs

DOCUMENT

Read the sections entitled "Survival of the Fittest" and "The Gospel of Wealth" on pages 528–531 of the text. The great industrialist Andrew Carnegie built his fortune on steel, but he also built a lasting reputation as a philanthropist because he spent millions of dollars on the establishment of libraries. Carnegie's *Gospel of Wealth* was a call for other rich people to share their wealth with the worthy poor. Consider the following questions: How does Carnegie's view exemplify Social Darwinism? What is the essence of Carnegie's argument against socialism? On what social values and assumptions about human nature was the gospel of wealth based?

The price which society pays for the law of competition, like the price it pays for cheap comforts and luxuries, is also great; but the advantages of this law are also greater still for it is to this law that we owe our wonderful material development, which brings improved conditions in its train. But, whether the law be benign or not, we must say of it as we say of the change in the conditions of men to which we have referred: It is here; we cannot evade it; no substitutes for it have been found; and while the law may be sometimes hard for the individual, it is best for the race, because it insures the survival of the fittest in every department. We accept and welcome, therefore, as conditions to which we must accommodate ourselves, great inequality of environment, the concentration of business, industrial and commercial, in the hands of a few, and the law of competition between these, as being not only beneficial, but essential for the future progress of the race. . . .

Objections to the foundations upon which society is based are not in order, because the condition of the race is better with these than it has been with any others which have been tried. Of the effect of any new substitutes proposed we cannot be sure. The Socialist or Anarchist who seeks to overturn present conditions is to be regarded as attacking the foundation upon which civilization itself rests, for civilization took its start from the day that the capable, industrious workman said to his incompetent and lazy fellow, "If dost not sew, thou shalt not reap," and thus ended primitive Communism by separating the drones from the bees. One who studies this subject will soon be brought face to face with the conclusion that upon the sacredness of property civilization *itself* depends—the right of the laborer to his hundred dollars in the savings bank, and equally the legal right of the millionaire to his millions. . . .

This, then, is held to be the duty of the man of Wealth: First, to set an example of modest, unostentatious living, shunning display or extravagance; to provide moderately for the legitimate wants of those dependent upon him; and after doing so to consider all surplus revenues which come to him simply as trust funds, which he is called upon to administer, and strictly bound as a matter of duty to administer in the manner which, in his judgment, is best calculated to produce the most beneficial results for the community—the man of wealth thus becoming the mere agent and trustee for his poorer brethren, bringing to their service his superior wisdom, experience, and ability to administer, doing for them better than they would or could do for themselves.

Andrew Carnegie, *The Gospel of Wealth* (1889).

MAP EXERCISE

Fill in or identify the following on the blank map provided.
1. Area of the early iron and steel industry.
2. Region of the early petroleum industry.

Interpretative Questions

Based on what you have filled in, answer the following. For some of the questions you will need to consult the narrative in your text for information or explanation.
1. Why did the Pullman railroad strike in the Chicago area disrupt the national transportation system to the extent that it did?
2. What factors combined to make the region from Pittsburgh to Chicago into America's industrial heartland?

SUMMARY

Although some economists place the industrial "takeoff" of America in the years before the Civil War, it was in the three decades following that great conflict that the United States became the world's leading industrial power. A fortunate combination of sufficient raw materials, adequate labor, enviable technological accomplishments, effective business leadership, nationwide markets, and supportive state and national governments boosted America past its international rivals. The industrial transformation had a profound impact on the lives of the millions of workers who made the production revolution possible. Some who were distrustful of industrial power turned toward socialism; others tried to organize workers into powerful unions. But in these early years of industrial conflict, the forces of business usually triumphed.

CHAPTER SELF-TEST

After you have read the chapter in the text and done the exercises in the study guide, the following self-test can be taken to see if you understand the material you have covered. Answers appear at the end of the study guide.

Multiple Choice

Circle the letter of the response that best answers the question or completes the statement.

1. The two methods of transforming iron into steel that emerged in the 1850s and 1860s were:
    a. the Cyrus-Field method and the air-jet process.
    b. the Bessemer-Kelly method and the open-hearth process.
    c. the Ritty-Scholes method and the molten-pot process.
    d. the Duryea-Thomas method and the ferrous-oxide process.

2. In the nineteenth century, the early petroleum industry concentrated in what states?
    a. Oklahoma, Texas, and Louisiana
    b. California and Arizona
    c. New York and New Jersey
    d. Pennsylvania, Ohio, and West Virginia
    e. Illinois, Wisconsin, and Michigan

3. The production of gasoline-powered automobiles began in the United States during the:
    a. 1870s.
    b. 1880s.
    c. 1890s.
    d. 1900s.
    e. 1910s.

4. Frederick Winslow Taylor's theory of "scientific management" advocated:
    a. making the workplace pleasant so that workers would have a good attitude and therefore be more productive.
    b. dividing workers into teams and having each team produce the entire product so that the workers would have a sense of pride.
    c. reorganizing the production process by subdividing tasks to speed up production and reduce the dependency on highly skilled workers.
    d. having employees assemble components at home, then bring them to the factory and be paid by the piece.

5. The popularization of mass production by moving assembly line is generally credited to:
    a. Henry Ford and the automobile industry.
    b. Guglielmo Marconi and the radio industry.
    c. the Wright Brothers and the airplane industry.
    d. William S. Burroughs and the adding machine industry.
    e. Charles F. Brush and the street light industry.

6. What legal principle was crucial to the ability of corporations to sell large amounts of stock to investors not directly involved in the business?
    a. Sovereign immunity
    b. Limited liability
    c. Joint tenancy
    d. Habeas corpus
    e. Power of attorney

7. Andrew Carnegie built his dominance in the steel industry by which business integration strategy?
    a. Vertical
    b. Horizontal
    c. Angular
    d. Radical

8. The enormously influential New York City banker who helped perfect the trust and created United States Steel from Carnegie Steel was:
   a. Commodore Vanderbilt.
   b. Gustavus Swift.
   c. Averill Harriman.
   d. John D. Rockefeller.
   e. J. P. Morgan.

9. Horatio Alger was famous for his books that:
   a. told of poor boys who found success through hard work, perseverance, and luck.
   b. argued that natural selection and survival of the fittest controlled the economic world as well as the natural world.
   c. proposed the "single tax" on unearned increment property as a panacea for the country's economic problems.
   d. described a utopian social order discovered in the year 2000 by a man who went into a hypnotic sleep in 1889.

10. In the late nineteenth century, the majority of working children were employed in:
    a. railroads.
    b. factories.
    c. agriculture.
    d. mining.
    e. domestic service.

11. The nation's first major national labor conflict was the:
    a. 1868 steel strike.
    b. 1872 coal strike.
    c. 1877 railroad strike.
    d. 1884 textile strike.
    e. 1893 oil strike.

12. The nation's first major national labor organization was the:
    a. National Union of Workers.
    b. Knights of Labor.
    c. American Federation of Labor.
    d. Congress of Industrial Organizations.
    e. Industrial Workers of the World.

13. The leader of the American Federation of Labor in the 1880s and 1890s was:
    a. Terence V. Powderly.
    b. Cyrus McCormick.
    c. Henry Clay Frick.
    d. Samuel Gompers.
    e. Eugene V. Debs.

14. In the mind of middle-class Americans, the code word for the labor radicalism and violence of the 1880s and 1890s was:
    a. communism.
    b. anarchism.
    c. socialism.
    d. liberalism.
    e. vigilantism.

15. The *two* major strikes of the 1890s that were marred by violence and that tainted the image of unions in public opinion were the (choose two letters):
    a. Homestead steel strike.
    b. Pinkerton textile strike.
    c. Molly Maguire coal strike.
    d. Pullman railroad strike.
    e. Drake oil strike.

True/False

Read each statement carefully. Mark true statements "T" and false statements "F."

___1.   The principal use of petroleum in the late nineteenth century was oil for lubrication of machines rather than fuel.

___2.   Due to overbuilding in the pre–Civil War era, the number of miles of railroad track in the United States actually declined from 1860 to 1900.

___3.   John D. Rockefeller began building Standard Oil by concentrating on the refining stage of the petroleum industry.

___4.   Although the term "trust" technically referred to a specific form of business organization, the term came to be generally applied to any great economic combination.

___5.   In the developing economy of the late nineteenth century the majority of business tycoons personified the "rags to riches" rise to wealth and power.

___6.   The "gospel of wealth" referred to the idea that the rich had a responsibility to use their money to promote social progress.

___7. The theory of Social Darwinism argued that great concentrations of wealth in the late nineteenth century violated the principles of evolution and that a great economic collapse was inevitable.

___8. Worker frustration with the problems of monopoly led to the formation of the Socialist Labor Party, which elected several congressmen from northeastern urban areas.

___9. By the 1890s more women were employed in factories than as domestic workers.

___10. Most European immigrants who came to the United States up to the 1880s arrived from northern Europe and the British Isles (Germany, England, Ireland, etc.), but by 1900 southern and eastern Europeans (Italians, Poles, Russians, Greeks, Slavs, etc.) dominated.

___11. In general, railroads, mining companies, and industrial employers tried to discourage the immigration of workers from Europe.

___12. With very few exceptions, in the period from 1870 to 1910 women were prohibited from working in factories.

___13. The American Federation of Labor stressed the idea of "one big union" for all workers while the Knights of Labor was a coalition of individual craft unions.

___14. Grover Cleveland refused to use federal troops in labor conflicts because he regarded such incidents as state matters.

___15. Many European immigrants came to the United States intending to work for a few years to earn some money and then return to Europe.

Review Questions

These questions are to be answered with essays. This will allow you to explore relationships among individuals, events, and attitudes of the period under review.

1. List the seven main factors that combined to produce America's impressive rise to industrial supremacy and explain how each one contributed to the mix.

2. Both the success-oriented novels of Horatio Alger and the utopian works of Edward Bellamy were best-sellers in late-nineteenth-century America. What might explain the seeming contradiction between Americans' desire to read about how great their country was and their desire to read about how much it needed to improve?

3. The so-called robber barons both praised unfettered free enterprise and tried to eliminate competition. How can these apparently conflicting ideologies be reconciled?
4. Why were most of the industrial and business developments described in this chapter concentrated in the Northeast and Midwest with the West and the South lagging?

CHAPTER EIGHTEEN

The Age of the City

OBJECTIVES

A thorough study of Chapter 18 should enable you to understand:
1. The patterns and processes of urbanization in late-nineteenth-century America.
2. The changes in the pattern of immigration in the late nineteenth century.
3. The new economic and social problems caused by urbanization.
4. The relationships of both urbanization and immigration to the rise of boss rule.
5. The early rise of mass consumption and its impact on American life, especially for women.
6. The changes in leisure and entertainment opportunities including organized sports, vaudeville, movies, and other activities.
7. The main trends in literature and art during the Gilded Age and early twentieth century.
8. The impact of the Darwinian theory of evolution on the intellectual life of America.
9. The profound new developments in American educational opportunities.

PERTINENT QUESTIONS

The New Urban Growth (pp. 545–549)

1. Compare and contrast rural and urban population growth from 1860 to 1910. What was the attraction of the city, and what were the main sources of urban growth?
2. How did the typical immigrants of the 1890s and later differ in ethnic background and economic status from most of the earlier immigrants?
3. How diverse was the immigration to the United States from 1860 to 1900?

4. What social institutions and community actions helped facilitate immigrants' adjustment to urban life in America?
5. Which immigrant groups adapted especially well economically? Which groups lagged? Why?
6. What attitudes and actions characterized the assimilation of first- and second-generation European immigrants?
7. What organizations and laws resulted from the resentment that many native-born Americans felt toward the new immigrants? What effect did the laws have?

The Urban Landscape (pp. 550–554)

8. What motives led to the movement for great urban parks, libraries, museums, and other public facilities in the late nineteenth century? What park became the standard?
9. How did large cities expand their boundaries and the land available for development in this period?
10. Compare and contrast the residential patterns of the wealthy and moderately well-to-do urbanites with those of the majority.
11. What was life like in the "tenements" of large American cities?
12. How did urban mass transportation technology evolve from omnibus to electric trolley?
13. What new construction technologies made the "skyscraper" possible?

Strains of Urban Life (pp. 555–558)

14. Describe the urban hazards of fire, disease, and sanitation and the public and private responses to them. What was the effect of the several great fires and disasters from 1871 to 1906?
15. What bred the increasing crime rate of late-nineteenth-century America? How did the cities respond? What similarities and differences can be seen between this period and the late twentieth century?
16. What factors contributed to the rise of political machines and their bosses? What were the positive as well as the negative aspects of boss rule in large cities?

The Rise of Mass Consumption (pp. 558–560)

17. Describe the changes in income and purchasing power of the urban middle and working classes. Who made the greater gains? Who lagged behind?
18. What changes marked the "new consumerism" for urban dwellers in the late nineteenth and early twentieth century?

What new developments in retailing accompanied the new consumerism?

19. How did the new consumerism impact life for American women —especially middle-class urban women?

Leisure in the Consumer Society (pp. 561–569)

20. How did turn-of-the-century Americans come to reconceptualize their idea of "leisure"? What examples manifest this change?

21. Compare and contrast the rise of baseball with that of football. What other spectator sports became popular as Americans came to enjoy more leisure time?

22. What were the main sorts of popular entertainment available to urban dwellers of the late nineteenth and early twentieth centuries? How did leisure activities bring people together? What barriers remained? How did Coney Island illustrate these developments?

23. What important changes occurred in journalism and publishing in the decades after the Civil War?

24. Describe the evolution of telephone technology from the 1870s to the early twentieth century. How did AT&T come to dominate the field?

High Culture in the Urban Age (pp. 569–576)

25. What issues did the realist novelists explore? Who were the leading realists?

26. How did Darwinism challenge traditional American faith and contribute to the growing schism between urban and rural values?

27. Describe the evolution of free public schooling in the United States. What parts of the nation lagged in education?

28. What government and private actions combined to lead the establishment of new universities and colleges and significant expansion of existing institutions after the Civil War?

29. What new attitudes, theories, and technologies helped America to move to the world's forefront in medical care?

30. What opportunities for higher education were available to women in this era? What were the distinctive characteristics of women's colleges, and how did they reflect other changes in women's organizations?

IDENTIFICATION

Identify each of the following, and explain why it is important within the context of the chapter.

1. "immigrant ghettoes"
2. Reform Judaism
3. American Protective Association/Immigration Restriction League
4. Frederick Law Olmstead
5. Columbian Exposition of 1893
6. "city beautiful" movement
7. Salvation Army
8. William M. Tweed
9. "white collar" workers
10. Cincinnati Red Stockings
11. James A. Naismith
12. Florenz Ziegfeld
13. minstrel shows
14. D. W. Griffith/*The Birth of a Nation*
15. "dime novels"
16. William Randolph Hearst
17. realism/Stephen Crane
18. John Singer Sargent
19. Ashcan School/Armory Show
20. pragmatism
21. Carlisle Indian Industrial School
22. G. W. Crile

DOCUMENT

Read the sections entitled "The New Urban Growth" and "The Urban Landscape" on pages 545–554 of the text and then read the excerpt below, taken from *How the Other Half Lives* (1890), the famous book by Jacob Riis. Consider the following questions: What comparisons could be made between the poor neighborhood of the late nineteenth century and that of today? What insights on assimilation does Riis offer?

> When once I asked the agent of a notorious Fourth Ward alley how many people might be living in it I was told: one hundred and forty families, one hundred Irish, thirty-eight Italian, and two that spoke the German tongue. Barring the agent herself, there was not a native-born individual in the court. The answer was characteristic of the cosmopolitan character of lower New York, very nearly so of the whole of it, wherever it runs to alleys and courts. One may find for the asking an Italian, a

German, a French, African, Spanish, Bohemian, Russian, Scandinavian, Jewish, and Chinese colony. Even the Arab, who peddles "holy earth" from the Battery as a direct importation from Jerusalem, has exclusive preserves at the lower end of Washington Street. The one thing you shall vainly ask for in the chief city of America is a distinctively American community. There is none; certainly not among the tenements.
. . .

The once-unwelcome Irishman has been followed in his turn by the Italian, the Russian Jew, and the Chinaman, and has himself taken a hand at opposition, quite as bitter and quite as ineffectual, against these later hordes. Wherever these have gone they have crowded him out, possessing the block, the street, the ward with their denser swarms. . . .

A map of the city, colored to designate nationalities, would show more stripes than the skin of a zebra, and more colors than any rainbow.

Jacob Riis, *How the Other Half Lives*.

MAP EXERCISE

Fill in or identify the following on the blank map provided.

1. Urban population centers of over one-half million (500,000) in 1900.

2. Smaller but more important regional cities: Buffalo; Cleveland; Detroit; Washington, D.C.; Atlanta; New Orleans; Memphis; Minneapolis; Cincinnati; Louisville; Kansas City; Dallas; Houston; Denver; Seattle; San Francisco; and Los Angeles.

3. The area of heaviest industrial concentration.

Interpretative Questions

Based on what you have filled in, answer the following. For some of the questions you will need to consult the narrative in your text for information or explanation.

1. Explain the relationships among railroads, industry, and large cities.
2. In what part of the nation, and specifically in what large cities, did the bulk of the post-1880 foreign immigrants settle?
3. Within the area indicated by the map as settled, which well-populated region of the country was most lacking in large cities of 100,000 or more? Why?
4. Note that all of the major urban areas of the late twentieth century were already established by 1900. What does this indicate about the maturity of the national economic and transportation system by the turn of the century?

SUMMARY

In the years after the Civil War, America's cities boomed as people left the rural areas of Europe and the United States to seek jobs and other attractions offered by American cities. The cities' rapid growth caused many problems in housing, transportation, and health. Technological attacks on these problems barely kept pace, and city governments often resorted to boss rule to cope. Immigrant groups fought for economic success, but groups that faced strong prejudices found it more difficult to advance than groups that did not. In addition to offering a new consumerism for many residents, the booming cities were places of intellectual ferment and cultural change. Many Americans wanted to prove to skeptical Europeans that the nation had cultural as well as economic accomplishments to admire. At the same time, American art and literature often continued to imitate European models. New medical advances made Americans healthier, and the nation's culture became more uniform through compulsory education, mass-market journalism, and standardized sports.

CHAPTER SELF-TEST

After you have read the chapter in the text and done the exercises in the study guide, the following self-test can be taken to see if you understand the material you have covered. Answers appear at the end of the study guide.

Multiple Choice

Circle the letter of the response that best answers the question or completes the statement.

1. Because of rapid growth in the latter nineteenth century, American cities:
   a. protected traditional social and cultural values.
   b. provided services and facilities inadequate to demands.
   c. witnessed the flight of factories and corporate offices to newer, less crowded locations.
   d. supported efficient and honest governments.

2. An important population trend that occurred in the United States from 1860 to 1910 was:
   a. a gradual decline of the rural population.
   b. the mass movement of urban population of all classes from city centers to suburbs.
   c. a population shift from the North to the South.
   d. a faster rate of growth for the cities than for the general population.

3. The movement of blacks from the rural South to industrial cities began during the latter nineteenth century because of :
   a. poverty and oppression in the South.
   b. prospective professional opportunities in the cities.
   c. the abundance of factory jobs in the North for blacks.
   d. the lack of racial discrimination in the North.

4. The new immigrants of the latter nineteenth century settled primarily in Eastern industrial cities because they:
   a. lacked the capital to buy land and begin farming in the West.
   b. found immediate employment as unskilled factory workers.
   c. found refuge and camaraderie among fellow nationals there.
   d. All of the above

5. The formation of ethnic neighborhoods by immigrants in American cities:
   a. tended to preserve significant aspects of the cultural values of their previous societies.
   b. resulted from discriminatory zoning restrictions.
   c. prevented their identification with and advancement in American society.
   d. intensified a sense of not belonging to a coherent community.

6. Nativist reaction against European immigrants of the latter nineteenth century resulted from all of the following factors *except* the:
   a. arrival of vast numbers of immigrants.
   b. refusal of most immigrant groups to try to assimilate themselves into American culture.
   c. generalized fears and prejudices against foreigners.
   d. economic concern that immigrant workers would threaten the wages and positions of American workers.

7. Which of the following was *not* a trend contributing to the rise of mass consumption in latter nineteenth-century America?
   a. The emergence of ready-made clothing as a basis of the American wardrobe.
   b. The breakup of marketing monopolies held by national chain stores.
   c. The development of canned food and refrigerated railroad cars.
   d. The emergence of great department stores and mail-order houses.

8. The emergence of national press services in the latter nineteenth century contributed significantly to:
   a. lower salaries for reporters since fewer were needed.
   b. more standardization of the news product.
   c. less separation of news from opinions.
   d. making newspapers more of a creative exercise and less of a business.

9. Which of the following was *not* part of the movement toward realism in literature?
   a. Stephen Crane
   b. Winslow Homer
   c. Upton Sinclair
   d. Kate Chopin

10. The theory of evolution:
    a. supported traditional American beliefs about the nature of man and history.
    b. met uniform resistance from middle-class Protestant religious leaders.
    c. gained greater acceptance in rural rather than urban areas.
    d. influenced new ways of thinking in the social sciences.

11. According to the philosophy of pragmatism, what should modern society rely on for guidance?
    a. Inherited ideals
    b. Scientific inquiry
    c. Moral principles
    d. Religious beliefs

12. Which of the following medical advances did *not* come into wide use in the late ninteenth and early twentieth centuries?
    a. Blood transfusion during surgery
    b. Diagnostic X-ray
    c. Asprin
    d. Organ transplants

13. Which of the following trends in American education did *not* take place in the latter nineteenth century?
    a. The spread of universal, free public education.
    b. Passage by states of compulsory attendance laws.
    c. Rapid proliferation of the nation's colleges.
    d. Increased emphasis on the classical curriculum at the university level.

14. Educational opportunities for women expanded in the post–Civil War era as:
    a. states used the Morrill Land Grant Act to create schools for women.
    b. a growing network of women's colleges resulted primarily from philanthropic donations.
    c. most state college systems promoted an ideal of coeducation.
    d. private universities admitted female students in a drive for sexual egalitarianism.

15. The Carlisle School was dedicated to the education of:
    a. women.
    b. Roman Catholics.
    c. American Indians.
    d. African Americans.

True/False

Read each statement carefully. Mark true statements "T" and false statements "F."

___1. Urban black males in the late nineteenth century usually held skilled industrial jobs.

___2. European immigrants to the United States, especially second- and third-generation individuals, staunchly resisted assimilation into the dominant culture.

___3. Political bosses and the machines they operated were usually more popular with people in the poor and working-class neighborhoods of large cities than with people of the upper and middle classes?

___4. The working class made greater income and lifestyle gains in the late nineteenth century than did the middle class.

___5. In the Gilded Age and the early twentieth century, baseball was more important as a college and university sport, and football was mainly played by professionals.

___6. The urban park movement, exemplified by Central Park in New York City, emulated formal European garden design concepts.

___7. The rapid industrial expansion of this period was accompanied by a work ethic that downplayed the importance of leisure as compared to the antebellum period.

___8. Darwinism was opposed by all organized Christian religious groups.

___9. Because of the lack of private schools available, the South led the nation in the establishment of tax-supported public schools for all children.

___10. By granting large amounts of land to state governments, the federal government encouraged states to establish universities and colleges that would emphasize practical learning, especially in agriculture and mechanics.

___11. Hundreds of thousands of European immigrants got their first taste of America as they were processed by customs at Coney Island in New York Harbor.

___12. Minstrel shows laid the foundation for the emergence of serious symphony orchestras in the early twentieth century.

___13. D. W. Griffith was a pioneer in the production of motion pictures.

___14. Jacob Riis was a journalist whose stories about life in urban slums helped inspire reformers.

___15. William Randolph Hearst was the founder of the "reform" movement within Judaism.

Review Questions

These questions are to be answered with essays. This will allow you to explore relationships among individuals, events, and attitudes of the period under review.

1. What factors combined to attract the great masses of people to the cities of America? What were the characteristics of these migrants?

2. Describe the problems created by the stunning pace at which American cities were growing. How well did the institutions of urban life respond to these problems?

3. Much of the serious art and literature of the late nineteenth and early twentieth centuries functioned as social criticism. Was the supposedly realistic criticism based on a balanced view of America's new urban culture?

4. In what ways did the "new consumerism" and new approaches to leisure pioneered in the late ninteenth and early twentieth centuries presage life in America a century later?

CHAPTER NINETEEN

From Stalemate to Crisis

OBJECTIVES

A thorough study of Chapter 19 should enable you to understand:

1. The limited role of the federal government and the nature of American party politics in the last third of the nineteenth century.
2. The problems of political patronage in the administrations of Rutherford B. Hayes, James A. Garfield, and Chester A. Arthur that led to the passage of the Pendleton Act.
3. The circumstances that permitted the Democrats to gain control of the presidency in the elections of 1884 and 1892.
4. The origins, purposes, and effectiveness of the Interstate Commerce Act and the Sherman Antitrust Act.
5. The position of the two major parties on the tariff question, and the actual trend of tariff legislation in the 1880s and 1890s.
6. The rise of agrarian discontent as manifested in the Granger movement, the Farmers' Alliances, and the Populist movement.
7. The rise of the silver question from the Crime of '73 through the Gold Standard Act of 1900.
8. The significance of the presidential campaign and election of 1896.

PERTINENT QUESTIONS

The Politics of Equilibrium (pp. 579–587)

1. How well balanced were the two major political parties between the Civil War and the turn of the century—especially from the mid-1870s to the early 1890s?
2. What explains the extraordinary loyalty that voters showed to their political parties in this period?
3. What regional, religious, and ethnic factors distinguished the two major parties?

4. What was the patronage system, and how did it dominate national politics in the 1870s and 1880s?

5. How was James A. Garfield a victim of the spoils (patronage) system?

6. What was the key issue in the 1888 presidential election? How was this campaign different from typical Gilded Age fare? What was done about the issue during the Benjamin Harrison administration? How did the same issue affect the 1890 and 1892 elections?

7. What led to passage of the Sherman Antitrust Act? What practical impact did it have?

8. What caused the demise of state-based railroad regulation? How was the demise related to the passage of the Interstate Commerce Act?

9. Why was the Interstate Commerce Commission so ineffectual?

The Agrarian Revolt (pp. 587–593)

10. Explain the evolution of purpose and the accomplishments of the Grange. Why did it eventually fail?

11. How did the Farmers' Alliance become transformed into the People's Party?

12. Who was most attracted to Populism? Why did the movement fail to obtain significant labor support?

13. What doomed the possibilities for effective biracial cooperation among Populists?

14. What did the Populists stand for and what were their leaders like? How, according to "Debating the Past" (p. 590), have historians differed in their interpretations of Populism?

The Crisis of the 1890s (pp. 593–601)

15. What were the immediate and long-range causes of the Panic of 1893? How serious was the depression that followed?

16. What developments after 1870 led to the coalition of farmers and miners on behalf of silver coinage?

17. Explain the debate over the gold standard. How did it divide the Democratic Party?

18. How did the nomination of William Jennings Bryan as the Democratic presidential candidate in 1896 put the Populists in a dilemma? How did they resolve it, and what was the result?

19. Describe the passions of the 1896 campaign. Where did Bryan do well? Why did he lose?

20. How did President William McKinley handle the bimetallism question? What happened during his administration to help resolve the issue?

IDENTIFICATION

Identify each of the following, and explain why it is important within the context of the chapter.
1. "Lemonade Lucy"
2. Civil War pensions
3. James G. Blaine
4. "rum, romanism, and rebellion"
5. James B. Weaver
6. Granger Laws
7. "Colored Alliances"
8. "subtreasuries"
9. Coxey's Army
10. 16:1
11. "Crime of '73"
12. "cross of gold"
13. Tom Watson

DOCUMENT

Probably the clearest expression of Populist goals was the Omaha platform of 1892, from which the following excerpt is taken. In light of this document, the text narrative, and the "Debating the Past" section on Populism, consider the following questions: Were the Populist demands reasonable and rational responses to the problems facing the Populist constituency? What elements of socialism can be found in the Populist program? How was the platform designed as an attempt to broaden the appeal of Populism beyond farmers?

We declare, therefore—

First.—That the union of the labor forces of the United States this day consummated shall be permanent and perpetual; may its spirit enter into all hearts for the salvation of the Republic and the uplifting of mankind.

Second.—Wealth belongs to him who creates it, and every dollar taken from industry without an equivalent is robbery. "If any will not work, neither shall he eat." The interests of rural and civil labor are the same; their enemies are identical.

Third.—We believe that the time has come when the railroad corporations will either own the people or the people must own the railroads; and should the government enter upon the work of owning and managing all railroads, we should favor an amendment to the constitution by which all persons engaged in government service shall be placed under a civil-service regulation of the most rigid character, so as to prevent the increase of power of the national administration by the use of such additional government employees.

FINANCE.—We demand a national currency, safe, sound, and flexible, issued by the general government only, a full legal tender for all debts, public and private, and that without the use of banking corporations; a just, equitable, and efficient means of distribution direct to the people, at a tax not to exceed 2 per cent, per annum, to be provided as set forth in the subtreasury plan of the Farmers' Alliance, or a better system; also by payments in discharge of its obligations for public improvements.

1. We demand free and unlimited coinage of silver and gold at the present legal ratio of 16 to 1.

2. We demand that the amount of circulating medium be speedily increased to not less than $50 per capita.

3. We demand a graduated income tax.

4. We believe that the money of the country should be kept as much as possible in the hands of the people, and hence we demand that all State and national revenues shall be limited to the necessary expenses of the government, economically and honestly administered.

5. We demand that postal savings banks be established by the government for the safe deposit of the earnings of the people and to facilitate exchange.

TRANSPORTATION.—Transportation being a means of exchange and a public necessity, the government should own and operate the railroads in the interest of the people. The telegraph and telephone, like the post-office system, being a necessity for the transportation of news, should be owned and operated by the government in the interest of the people.

LAND.—The land, including all the natural sources of wealth, is the heritage of the people, and should not be monopolized for speculative purposes, and alien ownership of land should be prohibited. All land now held by railroads and other corporations in excess of their actual needs, and all lands now owned by aliens; should be reclaimed by the government and held for actual settlers only.

Omaha Platform of the Populist Party, 1892.

MAP EXERCISE

Fill in or identify the following on the blank map provided.

1. The Great Plains, the silver mining regions, and the cotton-tobacco belt.

2. Territories not yet states as of 1896.

3. States carried by Bryan in the 1896 election.

Interpretative Questions

Based on what you have filled in, answer the following. For some of the questions, you will need to consult the narrative in your text for information or explanation.

1. Where was the Grange strongest? In what parts of the country did the Populist movement have the most impact? Why?

2. Why were the states carried by Bryan mainly those of the Great Plains, the silver mining regions, and the cotton-tobacco belt? Why did he fail to make inroads in the Midwest and Northeast?

SUMMARY

Close elections and shifting control of the White House and Congress characterized the politics of the period from 1876 to 1900. Regional, ethnocultural, and economic factors helped determine party affiliation, and elections often turned on considerations of personality. But there were real issues, too. Tariff, currency, and civil-service questions arose in almost every election. Discontented farmers in the People's Party briefly challenged the Republicans and Democrats, but the two-party system remained intact and the role of the federal government remained limited.

The election of 1896, the great battle between the gold standard and the silver standard, firmly established the Republican Party as the majority party in the United States. Agrarian and mining interests were unable to convince voters that currency inflation through the free coinage of silver would lead the nation out of the depression of the 1890s. By fusing with the Democrats, the Populists ended any chance they might have had to become a major force in American politics. By the end of the nineteenth century, business forces had triumphed. They had secured a gold-based currency and a rigorously protective tariff. Efforts to regulate railroads and trusts were halfhearted to begin with and were weakened even further by court decisions.

CHAPTER SELF-TEST

After you have read the chapter in the text and done the exercises in the study guide, the following self-test can be taken to see if you understand the material you have covered. Answers appear at the end of the study guide.

Multiple Choice

Circle the letter of the response that best answers the question or completes the statement.

1. Which of the following Americans would likely have voted Republican in the latter nineteenth century?
   a. A white Southern farmer
   b. A Northern Protestant industrialist
   c. A Catholic immigrant merchant
   d. A poor, urban factory worker

2. Following the Civil War, the leaders of both political parties seemed most concerned with:
   a. resolving the dispute between protectionists and advocates of free trade.
   b. providing inflation of the money supply.
   c. curbing the growing power of big business.
   d. winning elections and controlling patronage.

3. The Sherman Antitrust Act of 1890 was:
   a. passed by a narrow margin after a long and bitter debate in Congress.
   b. immediately successful in halting the trend toward business monopolization.
   c. intended by Congress to restructure the economy.
   d. virtually emasculated by hostile court decisions.

4. The Interstate Commerce Act of 1887 provided for:
   a. nominal government supervision of the railroads, designed principally to satisfy the popular clamor for reform.
   b. discrimination in railroad rates between long and short hauls.
   c. an objective standard to determine the extent to which railroad rates were "reasonable and just."
   d. an Interstate Commerce Commission with a clear authority to fix railroad rates.

5. Jacob S. Coxey:
   a. led a march on Washington to protest the depression of the 1890s and to make demands.
   b. organized Farmers' Alliance chapters across the South and Midwest.
   c. masterminded William McKinley's political career.
   d. wrote dozens of short novels about how millionaires went from "rags to riches."
   e. directed a massive public works program.
   f. advocated a reduction of the tariff.

6. Which of the following groups of the latter nineteenth century would *not* have favored an inflationary policy of "free silver" by the government?
   a. Bankers
   b. Silver miners
   c. Farmers
   d. Debtors

7. Helping William Jennings Bryan win the 1896 Democratic nomination for president was his:
   a. long record of distinguished congressional service.
   b. connection with the urban political machines.
   c. loyal defense of the Cleveland administration.
   d. dramatic "Cross of Gold" speech.

8. In the election of 1896, the Populists:
   a. named their own candidate and thus split the protest vote.
   b. approved William Jennings Bryan but nominated their own vice-presidential candidate.
   c. accepted complete "fusion" with the Democrats.
   d. lost much of their thunder with the adoption of a conservative platform.

9. William Jennings Bryan, in the election of 1896, was the first presidential candidate to:
   a. systematically "stump" every section of the nation.
   b. rely on a "front porch" strategy in meeting the voters.
   c. turn over management of his campaign to a political boss.
   d. raise over $5 million worth of campaign contributions.

10. In politics, "patronage" generally refers to:
   a. the tendency of politicians to talk down to the voters.
   b. the system of fixed bids, kickbacks, and bribes that officeholders took from constituents.
   c. the way that wealthy industrialists controlled the legislators.
   d. the process of awarding government jobs to supporters of the winning party.

11. The key issue debated in the 1888 presidential election campaign was:
   a. monopoly.
   b. tariff.
   c. civil service.
   d. race.

12. The Grange organization was designed to help:
   a. farmers.
   b. industrial workers.
   c. former slaves.
   d. recent immigrants.

13. The so-called Crime of '73 referred to:
   a. corruption in the Grant administration.
   b. the government decision to stop coining silver.
   c. the creation of the railroad monopoly.
   d. the removal of the barrier to Catholic immigration.

14. The "ratio of 16 to 1," which was important to the politics of the 1890s, referred to:
   a. the number of poor people for every one middle-class person.
   b. the way that southern states counted African Americans for the purposes of determining congressional representation.
   c. the profit that railroads made for each ton carried.
   d. the value of silver compared to the value of gold.

15. The Populists advocated:
    a. abolition of the income tax.
    b. stricter regulation of railroads.
    c. government ownership of all factories.
    d. the end of currency inflation.

True/False

Read each statement carefully. Mark true statements "T" and false statements "F."

___1. The Republican Party controlled both houses of Congress and the Presidency for all but four years from 1876 to 1896.

___2. Electoral turnout of eligible voters in the Gilded Age tended to be lower than it is today.

___3. The assassination of William McKinley by an office seeker provided impetus to the passage of the Civil Service Act.

___4. In general, Grover Cleveland favored lower tariffs.

___5. The Sherman Antitrust Act applied initially only to railroads.

___6. The so-called Granger Laws provided for state government regulation of railroads.

___7. The federal courts often overturned decisions of the Interstate Commerce Commission.

___8. The Farmers' Alliance organization provided the foundation from which the Populist Party emerged.

___9. There was a separate Farmers' Alliance organization, affiliated with the larger group, for African-American farmers.

___10. The Populists sought to build ties with industrial workers but were generally unsuccessful in doing so.

___11. Some southern Populists tried to build political connections with black farmers, but the efforts did not prove lasting.

___12. Among the causes of the Panic of 1893 was the overexpansion of railroad construction.

___13. Most industrialized nations of the world recognized *both* gold and silver as backing for their monetary systems.

___14. Although the Populists agreed with William Jennings Bryan on the silver issue, they refused to endorse him in 1896 because it would have meant the loss of their identity.

___15. In the 1896 election, William Jennings Bryan received most of his votes from the farming areas of the Midwest and mid-Atlantic states.

Review Questions

These questions are to be answered with essays. This will allow you to explore relationships among individuals, events, and attitudes of the period under review.

1. How much policy difference was there between the Republicans and the Democrats in the Gilded Age? What other factors distinguished the parties?

2. Compare and contrast the three major farm groups: the Grange, the Farmers' Alliances, and the Populists. Do you agree with historians who believe that Populism was a reasonable and realistic response to agrarian grievances?

3. In a series of cases, including the *Wabash* case and *United States v. E. C. Knight Company,* the United States Supreme Court severely restricted all efforts to regulate business. What logic did the Court use in these cases, and what effect did the decisions have on congressional action and on business?

4. How did the politics of Reconstruction impact the balance of partisan power in the elections from the 1870s through the 1890s?

CHAPTER TWENTY

The Imperial Republic

OBJECTIVES

A thorough study of Chapter 20 should enable you to understand:

1. The new Manifest Destiny, and how it differed from the old Manifest Destiny.
2. The objectives of American foreign policy at the turn of the century with respect to Europe, Latin America, and Asia.
3. The variety of factors that motivated the United States to become imperialistic.
4. The relationship between American economic interests, especially tariff policy, and developments in Hawaii and Cuba.
5. The causes of the Spanish-American War.
6. The military problems encountered in fighting the Spanish and, subsequently, the Filipinos.
7. The problems involved in developing a colonial administration for America's new empire.
8. The motives behind the Open Door notes and the Boxer intervention.
9. The nature of the military reforms carried out by Elihu Root following the Spanish-American War.

PERTINENT QUESTIONS

Stirrings of Imperialism (pp. 604–609)

1. What intellectual, economic, philosophical, and racial factors helped create a new national mood more receptive to overseas expansionism?
2. What developments in the late 1880s and mid-1890s demonstrated the increasing interest of the United States in Latin America?
3. Describe Hawaiian society before significant contact with Americans. How did planters and missionaries transform the islands?

216

4. How did Hawaii gradually get drawn into America's economic and political sphere? Was full annexation inevitable?

War with Spain (pp.609–619)

5. What were the causes of American involvement in Cuban affairs? How was American public opinion shaped on these issues?
6. What two incidents combined finally to pull the United States into war with Spain?
7. Describe the American plans and preparations for the Spanish-American War. Why was the "Splendid Little War" so short?
8. Describe the role that black soldiers played in the Spanish-American War. What tensions surfaced?
9. What were the results of George Dewey's Philippine attack?
10. Describe the U.S. sea and land operations at Cuba. How did the U.S. manage to win despite poor planning and organization?
11. Compare and contrast the development of Cuba and Puerto Rico before and after the Spanish-American War. What was the key to the Puerto Rican economy?
12. What were the basic terms of the Treaty of Paris?
13. What arguments were raised for and against imperialism in general and annexation of the Philippines in particular? Why did President McKinley favor annexation? What role did William Jennings Bryan play?

The Republic as Empire (pp. 619–624)

14. Did the Platt Amendment and American actions in Cuba violate the spirit of the ostensible reasons that the United States went to war? Explain.
15. Explain the goals and tactics of the Philippine War. Was American policy in the war a repudiation of the ideals that had led the United States to help Cuba secure its independence?
16. How was the Open Door policy calculated to provide maximum commercial and diplomatic advantage at minimum cost? What did the costs turn out to be?
17. What changes from 1900 to 1903 gave the United States a more modern military establishment?

IDENTIFICATION

Identify each of the following, and explain why it is important within the context of the chapter.

1. Alfred Thayer Mahan
2. Pan American Union
3. Pearl Habor
4. Queen Liliuokalani
5. Samoa
6. "yellow journalism"
7. *Cuba Libre*
8. George Dewey
9. Rough Riders
10. Lares Rebellion
11. Emilio Aguinaldo
12. William Howard Taft
13. Chinese "spheres of influence"
14. John Hay
15. Boxer Rebellion
16. Elihu Root

DOCUMENT

Read the text section entitled "Stirrings of Imperialism" (p. 604). The selection below is taken from an article by Senator Henry Cabot Lodge (R-Mass.) in the March 1895 issue of *Forum* magazine. In the second of his more than thirty years in the Senate, Lodge criticized President Cleveland for his failure to annex Hawaii and then stated his general position on American expansionism. Consider the following questions: What motives for imperialism are reflected in Lodge's article? How would Lodge's argument fit with that of the Social Darwinists? How much of Lodge's dream became reality during his long service in the Senate?

> In the interests of our commerce and of our fullest development, we should build the Nicaragua Canal, and for the protection of that canal and for the sake of our commercial supremacy in the Pacific we should control the Hawaiian Islands and maintain our influence in Samoa. England has studded the West Indies with strong places which are a standing menace to our Atlantic seaboard. We should have among those islands at least one strong naval station, and when the Nicaragua Canal is built, the island of Cuba, still sparsely settled and of almost unbounded fertility, will become to us a necessity. Commerce follows the flag, and we should build up a navy strong enough to give protection to Americans in every quarter of the globe and sufficiently powerful to put our coasts beyond the possibility of successful attack.

The tendency of modern times is toward consolidation. It is apparent in capital and labor alike, and it is also true of nations. Small states are of the past and have no future. The modern movement is all toward the concentration of people and territory into great nations and large dominions. The great nations are rapidly absorbing for their future expansion and their present defense all the waste places of the earth. It is a movement which makes for civilization and the advancement of the race. As one of the great nations of the world, the United States must not fall out of the line of march.

For more than thirty years we have been so much absorbed with grave domestic questions that we have lost sight of these vast interests which lie just outside our borders. They ought to be neglected no longer. They are not only of material importance but they are matters which concern our greatness as a nation and our future as a great example. They appeal to our national honor and dignity and to the pride of country and of race.

Henry Cabot Lodge, *Forum,* March 1895.

MAP EXERCISE

Fill in or identify the following on the blank map provided.

1. Cuba, Puerto Rico, Hawaii, Samoa, Midway, Guam, the Philippines, and Alaska.
2. The area of the Venezuelan border dispute.
3. The area of the Chinese coast that was divided into European spheres of influence.

Interpretative Questions

Based on what you have filled in, answer the following. For some of the questions you will need to consult the narrative in your text for information or explanation.

1. Why was the acquisition of Pacific islands so important to American trading and naval interests?
2. How were the annexation of the Philippines and the pronouncement of the Open Door policy related?
3. Why did the United States think its interests were at stake in the Venezuelan border controversy?
4. How did the freeing of Cuba and the acquisition of Puerto Rico secure American hegemony in the Caribbean Sea?

SUMMARY

Turning its interest from the continental United States to the world at large, America in the years after the Civil War fought a war with Spain and acquired a far-flung empire. By 1900, American possessions included Alaska, Hawaii, the Philippines, Puerto Rico, and a string of Pacific islands. In addition, Cuba was essentially an American protectorate. The nation was suddenly a world power with worldwide responsibilities and burdens. The empire had been acquired for economic and philosophical reasons. Expansionism could provide an outlet for a perceived glut of American goods and an arena in which to demonstrate the superiority of Western civilization. To accommodate its new role, the nation had to devise ways to improve its military establishment and govern its overseas territories.

CHAPTER SELF-TEST

After you have read the chapter in the text and done the exercises in the study guide, the following self-test can be taken to see if you understand the material you have covered. Answers appear at the end of the study guide.

Multiple Choice

Circle the letter of the response that best answers the question or completes the statement.

1. The new "Manifest Destiny" contrasted with the pre–Civil War version in that the new:
   a. was mostly free of the attitudes of racial and ethnic superiority that had characterized the old.
   b. concentrated on lands not geographically adjacent to territory already controlled by the United States.
   c. was patriotically motivated whereas the old was steeped in economic exploitation.
   d. tended to involve use of military force whereas such force had been avoided with the old.

2. The renewed American interest in expansionism by the 1890s stemmed partly from the:
   a. restoration of prosperity at home.
   b. fear that Europeans were gaining control of the world and its markets.
   c. resolution of domestic political conflicts.
   d. desire to settle America's frontier regions.

3. The annexation of Hawaii by the United States occurred as a result of:
   a. the request of American missionaries in the 1820s.
   b. negotiation of a treaty with King Kalakaua in 1887.
   c. the overthrow of Queen Liliuokalani by American businessmen in 1893.
   d. passage of a joint resolution by Congress in 1898.

4. The American public was outraged by publication of a letter from Dupuy de Lôme, Spanish minister to Washington, in which he:
   a. described President McKinley as a weak man.
   b. called all North Americans cowardly.
   c. defended Spain's brutal attacks on civilians.
   d. declared that Spain would launch terrorist attacks on the U.S. if the U.S. invaded Cuba.

5. According to the most recent evidence, the sinking of the American battleship *Maine* was probably the result of:
   a. an attack by a Spanish submarine.
   b. contact with a Spanish mine in Havana's harbor.
   c. sabotage by Cuban revolutionaries.
   d. an accidental explosion inside one of the engine rooms.

6. The Spanish-American War was marked by:
   a. a lack of public enthusiasm and military volunteers.
   b. more American lives lost to disease than battle.
   c. efficient mobilization of military supplies and services.
   d. protracted, bloody guerrilla struggles.

7. American capture of Santiago, Cuba, resulted when:
   a. General William R. Shafter ordered his forces to surround the city.
   b. Theodore Roosevelt led the Rough Riders in a reckless charge up Kettle Hill.
   c. members of two black infantry divisions secured San Juan Hill.
   d. the Spanish fleet, in an attempted escape from the city's harbor, was destroyed by a waiting American squadron.

8. Spain's defeat in the Spanish-American war resulted primarily from:
   a. great numerical superiority by the United States in ships, guns, and military personnel in Cuba.
   b. her own weakness and incompetence.
   c. British intervention on the part of the United States.
   d. the efficient planning and execution of American military strategies.

9. Following the war, what did President McKinley decide to do with the Phillipines?
   a. Annex them as a United States colony.
   b. Return them to Spain.
   c. Grant them independence.
   d. Provide for an international army of occupation.

10. All of the following arguments were made against United States annexation of the Philippines *except* that:
    a. "inferior" Asian races would "pollute" the American population.
    b. defense of the islands would prove costly and entangle America in foreign alliances.
    c. such a move would repudiate American principles of independence and self-reliance.
    d. control of the islands would necessitate American involvement in the Oriental trade.

11. In response to the Philippine insurrection, the United States:
    a. resorted to brutal tactics very similar to those for which it had denounced the Spanish in Cuba.
    b. negotiated a truce with rebel leader Emilio Aguinaldo.
    c. spent far less money and effort than had been necessitated by the Spanish-American War.
    d. decided to grant the islands immediate independence.

12. The Open Door policy with China was appealing to the United States because it:
    a. won ready approval from European interests with Chinese "spheres of influence."
    b. seemed to allow American trade in China without the need for a military presence or confrontation with other Western powers.
    c. tempered Chinese expansionist impulses.
    d. assured the United States a part of any future dismemberment of China.

13. The Boxer Rebellion was an uprising by:
    a. American sugar growers to take over the government of Hawaii.
    b. Panamanians to win control of the canal zone from Colombia.
    c. Chinese nationalists to expel the "foreign devils" who controlled the country's commerce.
    d. Filipino insurgents to win their independence from the United States.

14. Shortly after the end of the Spanish-American War the U.S. military establishment was:
    a. given a modern command structure.
    b. reduced to a nominal size since the Indians had been pacified and there was no longer a nearby external threat.
    c. restructured, with a shift away from an emphasis on naval power to an increased reliance on infantry forces.
    d. ignored except as a cozy place for ex-war heroes and political patronage.

15. The Platt Amendment had the effect of giving the United States:
    a. significant control over the affairs of Cuba.
    b. ownership of the Panama Canal zone.
    c. virtually unlimited access to the markets of Japan.
    d. a bigger role in internal European economic affairs.

True/False

Read each statement carefully. Mark true statements "T" and false statements "F."

___1. Joseph Pulitzer and William Randolph Hearst, alone among prominent American publishers, disdained the sensationalistic reporting of the Cuban revolution of the 1890s as practiced by the nation's "yellow press."

___2. The American attack on the Spanish fleet at Manila resulted in the most difficult and bloodiest engagement of the Spanish-American War.

___3. Black volunteers were accepted for service in the Spanish-American War and black regiments were used in the American invasion force.

___4. United States contact with Hawaii began well before the Civil War.

___5. The United States fought a brief naval war with England over the dispute concerning the border of Venezuela.

___6. By 1895 almost all the population of Hawaii's main islands was of European ancestry.

___7. The main trade commodity between the United States and Cuba was cotton.

___8. The Spanish-American War was called the "splendid little war" because almost everything went smoothly and efficiently.

___9. Theodore Roosevelt was a leader in the domestic opposition to the Spanish-American War.

___10. The largest ground encounter of the Spanish-American War actually occurred in the Dominican Republic.

___11. Emilio Aguinaldo was the principal leader of the Cuban nationalists until he died in a detention camp prior to American intervention.

___12. Chinese "spheres of influence" referred to those Pacific islands, including Samoa, where the United States had interests that were dominated by the Chinese navy.

___13. Alfred Thayer Mahan was the key leader of the anti-imperialist movement that tried to prevent U.S. annexation of Hawaii and the Philippines.

___14. George Dewey led the American naval force that captured Manila Bay.

___15. When Puerto Rico was declared to be a U.S. territory and its residents were granted U.S. citizenship, all agitation for statehood or independence ended.

Review Questions

These questions are to be answered with essays. This will allow you to explore relationships among individuals, events, and attitudes of the period under review.

1. Compare and contrast the new and old concepts of Manifest Destiny. Look especially at the economic, philosophical, and racial motives for overseas expansion. Were these factors at work in the older continental expansionism?

2. What hesitations and doubts about imperialism did Americans evince between 1865 and 1898? How did the Spanish-American War change all this?
3. Was the Spanish-American conflict indeed a "splendid little war"? What was splendid about it? What was not so splendid?
4. What parallels can be drawn between America's imperial aspirations and the way white Americans dealt with the American Indian?

CHAPTER TWENTY-ONE

The Rise of Progressivism

OBJECTIVES

A thorough study of Chapter 21 should enable you to understand:
1. The origins of the progressive impulse.
2. The humanitarian reforms of the period, and the role of the church in carrying out the "Social Gospel."
3. The progressive emphasis on scientific expertise, organizational reform, and professionalism.
4. The role of women's groups in promoting reform.
5. The aims and accomplishments of the progressives at the state and local levels.
6. The temperance movement, and its relationship to other progressive reforms.
7. The movement to restrict immigration, and how allowing fewer immigrants was regarded as a reform.
8. The woman suffrage movement and more radical demands for equal rights for women.
9. The progressive attitude toward the consolidation of economic power in corporations.

PERTINENT QUESTIONS

The Progressive Impulse (pp. 629–635)

1. How did the muckrakers help prepare the way for progressivism?
2. What contribution did the Social Gospel movement make to progressivism?
3. How did the settlement house movement illustrate the progressive belief that the environment shaped individual development?
4. What distinguished the so-called new middle class? What was the role of expertise and professional organization? Who was usually excluded?

5. In what professions did women dominate? What characteristics did those professions share?

Women and Reform (pp. 636–640)

6. What basic change in the nature of the economy laid the foundation for the emergence of the so-called new woman? What were the characteristics of the new woman?

7. What led to the prominence of women in reform movements? How did the women's club movement reflect both the influence of women and the restrictions upon them?

8. What were the principal arguments for and against the woman suffrage movement? Why did the movement inspire such passionate antisuffrage sentiments?

9. Explain how the debate over the "sphere" of women shaped the suffrage movement. What shift in emphasis was critical in finally obtaining the vote for women?

The Assault on the Parties (pp. 640–645)

10. Explain how the commission plan, the city-manager plan, nonpartisanship, at-large elections, and stronger mayors worked together to try to destroy the power of the urban party bosses. Who supported such reforms? Who usually opposed them?

11. What were the basic purposes of the initiative, the referendum, the recall, and the direct primary? How widely were they adopted?

12. What was the relationship between the weakening of political parties and the rise of interest groups?

Sources of Progressive Reform (pp. 645–648)

13. What role did labor unions play in progressive reform? Why was the American Federation of Labor not involved at the national level?

14. By what means did some urban political machines, such as Tammany Hall, manage to survive the progressive era?

15. Why were western reformers particularly interested in action at the federal level even though much of the progressive movement focused on state and local legislation? What changes were accomplished?

16. Compare and contrast the ideas of Booker T. Washington with those of W. E. B. Du Bois. What was the organizational result of the efforts of Du Bois and his allies?

Crusades for Order and Reform (pp. 649–654)

17. Today, antiliquor laws are often thought of as conservative. Why was prohibition regarded as a progressive issue? What forces usually opposed prohibition?
18. Most progressives abhorred the urban disorder resulting from the influx of immigrants, but they differed about the appropriate response to the problem. What were the contrasting approaches? Which one dominated?
19. How did the socialist agenda differ from the typical progressive program? On what issues did the socialists disagree among themselves?
20. Describe the two different progressive approaches to the perceived problem of economic consolidation and centralization. What solutions did advocates of each approach favor?

IDENTIFICATION

Identify each of the following, and explain why it is important within the context of the chapter.
1. Lincoln Steffens
2. Salvation Army
3. *In His Steps*
4. Jane Addams
5. Thorstein Veblen
6. Taylorism
7. social science
8. American Medical Association
9. U.S. Chamber of Commerce
10. National Farm Bureau Federation
11. "Boston marriages"
12. General Federation of Women's Clubs
13. National Association of Colored Women
14. Carrie Chapman Catt and Anna Howard Shaw
15. Alice Paul
16. secret ballot
17. Robert M. La Follette
18. Triangle Shirtwaist Co. fire
19. Niagara Movement
20. Women's Christian Temperance Union
21. Frances Willard
22. eugenics

23. Eugene V. Debs
24. Industrial Workers of the World
25. Louis D. Brandeis

DOCUMENT

Read the text section entitled "Woman Suffrage"(p. 638). The document below is drawn from a flyer published in 1905 by the Anti-Suffrage Association, based in Albany, New York. The pamphlet was written by noted historian Francis Parkman and was issued several years after his death. Consider the following questions: Why would the emphasis on the "natural" way have been an effective argument against suffrage? To what extent was the suffrage fight a battle among women as well as between men and women? How do Parkman's arguments compare with those who opposed the Equal Rights Amendment in the 1970s and 1980s?

The man is the natural head of the family, and is responsible for maintenance and order. Hence he ought to control the social and business agencies which are essential to the successful discharge of the trust imposed upon him. . . .

Woman suffrage must have one of two effects. If, as many of its advocates complain, women are subservient to men, and do nothing but what they desire, then woman suffrage will have no other result than to increase the power of the other sex; if, on the other hand, women vote, as they see fit, without regarding their husbands, ... then unhappy marriages will be multiplied and divorces redoubled. . . .

But most women, including those of the best capacity and worth, fully consent that their fathers, husbands, brothers, or friends, shall be their political representatives. . . .

Nothing is more certain than that woman will have the suffrage if they ever want it; for when they want it, men will give it to them regardless of consequences. . . .

Many women of sense and intelligence are influenced by the fact that the woman suffrage movement boasts itself a movement of progress, and by a wish to be on the liberal or progressive side. But the boast is unfounded. Progress, to be genuine, must be in accord with natural law. If it is not, it ends in failure and in retrogression. . . .To plunge [women] into politics, where they are not needed and for which they are unfit, would be scarcely more a movement of progress than to force them to bear arms and fight. . . .

Neither Congress, nor the States, nor the united voice of the whole people could permanently change the essential relations of the sexes. Universal female suffrage, even if decreed, would undo itself in time; but the attempt to establish it would work deplorable mischief. The question is, whether the persistency of a few agitators shall plunge us blindfold into the most reckless of all experiments; whether we shall adopt this supreme device for developing the defects of women, and demolish their real power to build an ugly mockery instead. For the sake of womanhood, let us hope not. . . .Let us save women from the barren perturbations of American politics. Let us respect them; and, that we may do so, let us pray for deliverance from female suffrage.

Francis Parkman, "Some of the Reasons Against Women's Suffrage" (Albany, N.Y.: Anti-Suffrage Association, 1905).

MAP EXERCISE

Fill in or identify the following on the blank map provided.

1. State known as "the laboratory of progressivism."
2. City in which Hull House was located.
3. Two cities that launched the commission form of municipal government.
4. Two states that did not ratify the Eighteenth Amendment, which established the prohibition of liquor.

Interpretative Questions

Based on what you have filled in, answer the following. For some of the questions you will need to consult the narrative in your text for information or explanation.

1. What led one state to be called the "laboratory of progressivism"? Who was this state's leading progressive?
2. In general, where were settlement houses located and why? What was their function? Why was Hull House the most famous settlement house in the United States?
3. What natural event in what city was the catalyst for the invention of the commission plan of municipal government? Note that both the commission plan and the manager plan began in small southern cities and only spread after they were adopted by larger northern cities. What factors would help explain this pattern?
4. What probably explains why the particular two states failed to ratify the Eighteenth Amendment?

SUMMARY

Convinced that rapid industrialization and urbanization had created serious problems and disorder, progressives shared an optimistic vision that organized private and government action could improve society. Progressivism sought to control monopoly, build social cohesion, and promote efficiency. Muckrakers exposed social ills that Social Gospel reformers, settlement house workers, and other progressives attacked. Meanwhile, increasing standards of training and expertise were creating a new middle class of educated professionals, including many women. The progressives tried to rationalize politics by reducing the influence of political parties in municipal and state affairs. Many of the nation's problems could be solved, some progressives believed, if alcohol were banned, immigration were restricted, and women were allowed to vote. With only scant help from white progressives, African Americans laid the organizational groundwork for attacks on racial discrimination. Other progressives stressed the need for fundamental economic transformation through socialism or through milder forms of antitrust action and regulation.

CHAPTER SELF-TEST

After you have read the chapter in the text and done the exercises in the study guide, the following self-test can be taken to see if you understand the material you have covered. Answers appear at the end of the study guide.

Multiple Choice

Circle the letter of the response that best answers the question or completes the statement.

1. Progressive reforms were shaped by a belief in the:
   a. need to concentrate power, wealth, and authority for the well-being of the nation.
   b. autonomy of the individual.
   c. laissez-faire orthodoxies of the late nineteenth century.
   d. importance of organization and efficiency.

2. The Social Gospel:
   a. helped bring a powerful moral component to progressivism.
   b. became the dominant philosophy in urban reform.
   c. was dismissed by serious reformers as irrelevant moralization.
   d. was rejected as materialistic by Pope Leo XIII.

3. Most progressive theorists argued that ignorance, poverty, and even criminality resulted from:
   a. a person's "fitness" for survival.
   b. inherent moral or genetic failings.
   c. the workings of divine providence.
   d. the effects of an unhealthy environment.

4. The high value placed by progressives on knowledge and expertise led to the:
   a. justification by middle-class professionals of the existing industrial system.
   b. use of scientific techniques in the study of society and its institutions.
   c. abandonment by managers of the principles of "Taylorism."
   d. rejection of mass-production techniques, such as the assembly line, in favor of highly skilled and trained laborers.

5. Professional roles for women in the early twentieth century were:
   a. widely expanded by custom and law into virtually every field of work.
   b. restricted entirely to the settlement houses and social work.
   c. free of the organizational trends characterizing the male professional world.
   d. most often those involving "helping" or "domestic" activities traditionally associated with women.

6. Women's clubs formed in the latter nineteenth and early twentieth centuries:
   a. confined their activities to social and cultural activities.
   b. seldom adopted positions on controversial public issues.
   c. overtly challenged the prevailing assumptions about the proper role of women in society.
   d. played an important role in winning passage of state laws regulating conditions of housing and the workplace.

7. To improve municipal government, many urban political reformers favored:
   a. election of mayors and other offices on a nonpartisan basis.
   b. movement of city elections to years of presidential or congressional contests.
   c. election of city councilors by district.
   d. increased power for the city council at the expense of the mayor.

8. Partly in response to progressive political reforms, the:
   a. power of party organizations collapsed.
   b. turnout of eligible voters increased.
   c. influence of special interest groups increased.
   d. influence of party bosses disappeared.

9. By the early twentieth century, the Women's Christian Temperance Union (WCTU):
   a. was widely ridiculed by most progressives as a collection of busybodies and do-gooders.
   b. demanded the complete prohibition of the manufacture and sale of alcoholic beverages.
   c. won substantial support from immigrants and working-class voters.
   d. remained a model of administrative inefficiency and political ineptitude.

10. The sources of greatest immigration to the United States from 1900 to 1920 were:
    a. Ireland and Germany.
    b. Italy and the Austro-Hungarian Empire.
    c. Russia and the Baltic states.
    d. China and Japan.

11. All of the following were movements advocated by many who called themselves progressive era reformers *except:*
    a. eliminating alcohol from national life.
    b. stopping the flood of immigrants.
    c. winning women the right to vote.
    d. abolishing child labor.
    e. prohibiting workers from joining unions.

12. The advocates of woman suffrage significantly increased their general public support during the progressive era when they put increased emphasis on the argument that woman suffrage would:
    a. lead to full social and economic power for women within a generation.
    b. increase political power and office-holding opportunities available to women.
    c. bring more women into the industrial work force thereby countering recession.
    d. enhance the likelihood of the successful enactment of other progressive reform causes.

13. In congressional and presidential circles, the central economic debate of the progressive era was whether the:
    a. unionization of workers should proceed along industrial or craft lines.
    b. capitalistic structure of the system should be replaced by socialism.
    c. government should deal with the trusts through policies of decentralization or regulation.
    d. government should rely primarily upon the tariff or income tax as the major source of revenue.

14. The leading American socialist of the progressive era was
    a. Herbert Croly.
    b. Louis D. Brandeis
    c. Alice Paul.
    d. Eugene V. Debs

15. Which of the following was a governor and United States senator regarded as a leading progressive?
    a. Chapman Catt
    b. Howard Shaw
    c. Robert La Follette
    d. Charles Tammany

True/False

Read each statement carefully. Mark true statements "T" and false statements "F."

___1. "Muckraker" was the nickname given by progressives to politicians who were accused of bribery and corruption.

___2. As a general rule, progressive reformers opposed placing governmental power in the hands of nonpartisan, nonelective bureaucrats, who were insulated from electoral politics.

___3. The adoption by many American cities of the commission and city-manager systems of municipal government signaled an attempt to remove municipal government from the corrupting influence of party politics.

___4. As a general rule, Social Darwinists stressed the role of inherent characteristics and progressives stressed the role of environment in explaining why poor people failed to succeed economically.

___5. The settlement house movement led by Jane Addams provided an opportunity for educated women to get together in a rural environment for intellectually stimulating retreats.

___6. Professional women who entered the work force during the progressive era tended to be concentrated in the so-called helping professions such as teaching and nursing.

___7. The women's club movement provided opportunities for women to exert influence on political issues as well as providing a social outlet.

___8. The electoral devices of initiative, referendum, and direct primary were instituted in several states in order to give more political power to the average voter rather than the incumbent legislators.

___9. The electoral device known as the "recall" allowed voters to remove an elected officeholder without waiting for the normal end of his term of office.

___10. In general, the increasing influence of interest groups during the progressive era strengthened the power of the two political parties.

___11. In general, opposition to prohibition of alcoholic beverages was weakest in the urban areas of the northeastern states.

___12. America's entry into World War I and the moral fervor it unleashed helped provide the final push for the adoption of the national prohibition of alcoholic beverages.

___13. Booker T. Washington's rhetoric tended to emphasize immediate economic self-improvement rather than long-range social change.

___14. The so-called science of eugenics was used by factory reformers to justify improved health and safety conditions and to call for increased education for the workers.

___15. Many progressives, such as Herbert Croly and Theodore Roosevelt, argued that national economic regulation was the best way to deal with the challenges brought forward by the trusts.

Review Questions

These questions are to be answered with essays. This will allow you to explore relationships among individuals, events, and attitudes of the period under review.

1. Consider the "central assumptions" of progressivism identified by the chapter introduction in light of the varying interpretations offered in the "Debating the Past" section on p. 650. Was progressivism unified enough to share "central assumptions"?

2. Many progressives professed to believe that government at all levels should be strong, efficient, and democratic so that it could better serve the people. What changes in the structure and

operation of government did progressives advocate to achieve these aims? Can the attempts at civil-service reform in the nineteenth century be seen as a precursor of this type of progressive program?

3. To what extent did muckrakers, Social Gospel reformers, settlement house volunteers, social workers, and other experts reflect the central assumptions of progressivism? How did those assumptions compare with Social Darwinistic ideas?

4. Explain how progressivism affected women and, conversely, how women affected progressivism.

CHAPTER TWENTY-TWO

The Battle for National Reform

OBJECTIVES

A thorough study of Chapter 22 should enable you to understand:

1. The nature and extent of Theodore Roosevelt's "square deal" progressivism.
2. The similarities and differences between the domestic progressivism of William Howard Taft and of Roosevelt.
3. The conservation issue, and why it triggered the split between Taft and Roosevelt.
4. The consequences of the split in the Republican Party in 1912.
5. The differences between Roosevelt's New Nationalism and Wilson's New Freedom.
6. The differences between Woodrow Wilson's campaign platform and the measures actually implemented during his term.
7. The new tone for American foreign policy introduced by Roosevelt, especially in Asia and the Caribbean.
8. The similarities and differences between Taft's and Roosevelt's approach to foreign policy.
9. The reasons for the continuation of American interventionism in Latin America under Wilson.

PERTINENT QUESTIONS

Theodore Roosevelt and the Progressive Presidency
(pp. 658–662)

1. How did Theodore Roosevelt become president?
2. To what extent was Roosevelt a trustbuster? What was Roosevelt's view about how the federal government should deal with economic concentration?
3. What changes did Roosevelt initiate in the traditional role of the federal government in labor disputes?

4. How did Roosevelt's actions in conservation and in the railroad, medicine, and meat industries illustrate his cautious but progressive approach?
5. How did Roosevelt respond to the Panic of 1907?

The Troubled Succession (pp. 662–666)

6. Contrast the personalities of Theodore Roosevelt and William Howard Taft. What seemed to be Taft's biggest problem?
7. How did Taft manage to alienate progressives on the tariff issue?
8. How did the Pinchot-Ballinger affair drive a wedge between Taft and Roosevelt?
9. Describe the programs that Roosevelt unveiled at Osawatomie, Kansas. How did they go beyond the moderation he had exhibited as president?
10. How did Taft manage to secure the Republican nomination in 1912 despite Roosevelt's obvious popularity?
11. Why did Roosevelt break from the Republicans to form the Progressive Party?

Woodrow Wilson and the New Freedom (pp. 666–670)

12. How did Roosevelt's New Nationalism and Wilson's New Freedom differ from each other?
13. What propelled Wilson to victory in 1912? What roles did Taft and Eugene Debs play in the campaign?
14. How did Wilson influence Congress to pass his legislative program?
15. What was the goal of the Underwood-Simmons tariff? How did it fulfill longstanding Democratic pledges? Why was a graduated income tax needed, as well as the tariff reduction?
16. How did the Federal Reserve Act transform the nation's monetary system?
17. Wilson pushed hard for the Federal Trade Commission Act and gave only lukewarm support to the Clayton Act. What do those actions demonstrate about his ironic move in the direction of New Nationalism?
18. After the initial spate of New Freedom legislation, how and why did Wilson back away from reform? What led him, later in his first term, to advance reform once again?

The "Big Stick": America and the World, 1901–1917
(pp. 670–678)

19. Explain Roosevelt's distinction between "civilized" and "uncivilized" nations. How did sea power fit into his vision?
20. What was the course of relations between the United States and Japan during Roosevelt's presidency?
21. What were the general and immediate motivations for the proclamation of the Roosevelt Corollary? What pattern of Latin American policy and intervention did it establish?
22. Why have many observers questioned the propriety of the methods that the United States used to acquire rights to construct the Panama Canal?
23. What was the central focus of William Howard Taft's foreign policy? What nickname was it given?
24. What were Wilson's actions in the Dominican Republic, Haiti, and Nicaragua? Were they consistent with the Roosevelt Corollary?
25. Why did Wilson take sides in the Mexican governmental turmoil? Describe the two interventions and their results.

IDENTIFICATION

Identify each of the following, and explain why it is important within the context of the chapter.

1. Seventeenth Amendment
2. Northern Securities case
3. Alton B. Parker
4. "square deal"
5. *The Jungle*
6. J. P. Morgan
7. William Jennings Bryan
8. Robert La Follette
9. "Bull Moose" party
10. Col. Edward M. House
11. Louis Brandeis
12. Sixteenth Amendment
13. Smith-Lever Act
14. Great White Fleet
15. Platt Amendment
16. Pancho Villa
17. John J. Pershing

DOCUMENT

Read the text section entitled "The Square Deal" p. 660. Also review earlier parts of the text that discuss the rise of big business and the role of corporate leadership. The following excerpts are from Theodore Roosevelt's first annual message, delivered only a few months after he became president. Read the selection and consider the following questions: Does this message reveal an attitude toward trusts consistent with the actions that Roosevelt would undertake as president? How might Roosevelt have reacted to those who called the great industrial leaders "robber barons"? Would this document support the contention that progressivism can best be explained as a reaction to the economic changes of the late nineteenth century? Are Roosevelt's views more consistent with those of Herbert Croly or Louis Brandeis? Does the Republican Party of today reflect a similar outlook toward business? Could it be fairly characterized as a "trickle-down" view?

> The tremendous and highly complex industrial development which went on with ever accelerated rapidity during the latter half of the nineteenth century brings us face to face, at the beginning of the twentieth, with very serious social problems. The old laws, and the old customs which had almost the binding force of law, were once quite sufficient to regulate the accumulation and distribution of wealth. Since the industrial changes which have so enormously increased the productive power of mankind, they are no longer sufficient.
>
> The growth of cities has gone on beyond comparison faster than the growth of the country, and the upbuilding of the great industrial centers has meant a startling increase, not merely in the aggregate of wealth, but in the number of very large individual, and especially of very large corporate, fortunes. The creation of these great corporate fortunes has not been due to the tariff nor to any other governmental action, but to natural causes in the business world operating in other countries as they operate in our own.
>
> The process has aroused much antagonism, a great part of which is wholly without warrant. It is not true that as the rich have grown richer the poor have grown poorer. On the contrary, never before has the average man, the wage-worker, the farmer, the small trader, been so well off as in this country at the present time. There have been abuses connected with the accumulation of wealth; yet it remains true that a fortune accumulated in legitimate business can be accumulated by the person specifically benefitted only on condition of conferring immense incidental benefits upon others. Successful enterprise, of the type which benefits all mankind, can only exist if the conditions are such as to offer great prizes as the rewards of success.
>
> The captains of industry who have driven the railway systems across this continent, who have built up our commerce, who have developed our manufactures, have on the whole done great good to our people. Without them the material development of which we are so justly proud could never have taken place. . . .
>
> Moreover, it cannot too often be pointed out that to strike with ignorant violence at the interests of one set of men almost inevitably endangers the interests of all. The fundamental rule in our national life—the rule which underlies all others—is that, on the whole, and in the long run, we shall go up or down together. . . .

The mechanism of modern business is so delicate that extreme care must be taken not to interfere with it in a spirit of rashness or ignorance. Many of those who have made it their vocation to denounce the great industrial combinations which are popularly, although with technical inaccuracy, known as "trusts," appeal especially to hatred and fear. These are precisely the two emotions, particularly when combined with ignorance, which unfit men for the exercise of cool and steady judgment. In facing new industrial conditions, the whole history of the world shows that legislation will generally be both unwise and ineffective unless undertaken after calm inquiry and with sober self-restraint. . . .

All this is true; and yet it is also true that there are real and grave evils, one of the chief being over-capitalization because of its many baleful consequences; and a resolute and practical effort must be made to correct these evils.

There is a widespread conviction in the minds of the American people that the great corporations known as trusts are in certain of their features and tendencies hurtful to the general welfare.

MAP EXERCISE

Fill in or identify the following on the blank map provided. Use the map on page 672 of the text as your source.

1. Mexico, Cuba, Haiti, Dominican Republic, Puerto Rico, Virgin Islands, Nicaragua, Panama, Venezuela, Colombia. (Mark a star on those countries into which the United States intervened militarily. Mark "RC" on the country to which the Roosevelt Corollary was first applied.)
2. Area of Pancho Villa's raids and General John J. Pershing's intervention.
3. The route of the Panama Canal.

Based on what you have filled in, answer the following. For some of the questions you will need to consult the narrative in your text for information or explanation.

1. Explain the motivation for Theodore Roosevelt's special concern with the Caribbean region. What policy did he formulate in response to his concerns?
2. What were the two possible routes for a Central American canal? What were the advantages and disadvantages of each? Why did the United States settle on the Panamanian choice? Why was Colombia upset?
3. What events inspired U.S. intervention in Nicaragua? Why was the country perceived to be important to American interests?
4. What caused the border strife between the United States and Mexico? What was its result?

SUMMARY

Theodore Roosevelt became president as a consequence of the assassination of William McKinley, but he quickly moved to make the office his own. In many ways, Roosevelt was the preeminent progressive, yet it sometimes seemed that for him reform was more a style than a dogma. Although Roosevelt clearly envisioned a more activist national government, the shifts and contractions embodied in his policies toward trusts, labor, and conservation reflect the complexity and diversity of progressivism. Despite being Roosevelt's handpicked successor, President William Howard Taft managed to alienate Roosevelt and other progressive Republicans by his actions regarding tariffs, conservation, foreign policy, trusts, and other matters. In 1912, Roosevelt decided to challenge Taft for the presidency. When he failed to secure the Republican nomination, Roosevelt formed his own Progressive Party. With the Republicans divided, Woodrow Wilson won the presidency. In actuality, Wilson's domestic program turned out to be much like the one Roosevelt had advocated. In the Caribbean, Wilson continued the pattern of intervention that Roosevelt and Taft had established.

CHAPTER SELF-TEST

After you have read the chapter in the text and done the exercises in the study guide, the following self-test can be taken to see if you understand the material you have covered. Answers appear at the end of the study guide.

Multiple Choice

Circle the letter of the response that best answers the question or completes the statement.

1. As president, Theodore Roosevelt:
   a. failed to attract significant public attention or devotion.
   b. openly rebelled against the conservative leaders of his party.
   c. advocated reform as a means of protecting American society against more radical challenges.
   d. earned a reputation for the substance, rather than the style, of his leadership.

2. In managing the trusts, Theodore Roosevelt advocated:
   a. government prosecution and breakup of only the largest trusts.
   b. regulation, with government serving as mediator between corporate and public interest.
   c. reversal of the prevailing trend toward economic concentration.
   d. strict enforcement of the Sherman Antitrust Act.

3. In contrast to Roosevelt, William Howard Taft was:
   a. more committed to progressive reform.
   b. insistent upon observing the strict letter of the law.
   c. dynamic and aggressive in personality.
   d. an ardent sportsman and athlete.

4. As president, Taft:
   a. lobbied effectively for reduced tariff rates.
   b. actively supported the insurgent revolt in Congress.
   c. refused to intervene in legislative affairs.
   d. successfully challenged the power of the conservative Old Guard.

5. The election of 1912 offered American voters a choice between:
   a. conservatism and reform.
   b. two brands of progressivism.
   c. socialism and capitalism.
   d. All of the above

6. Wilson perceived his role as president as one in which he should:
   a. deal primarily with foreign rather than domestic problems.
   b. delegate most authority to capable subordinates.
   c. guide public demands into legislative realities.
   d. remain above the political squabbles in Congress.

7. In contrast to earlier statements, as president, Woodrow Wilson seemed most supportive of:
   a. vigorous enforcement of the antitrust laws.
   b. additional legislation designed to dismantle the trusts.
   c. creation of a government regulatory agency for big business.
   d. policies to restore a competitive, decentralized economy.

8. The conduct of foreign affairs appealed to Theodore Roosevelt because there the president:
   a. met a lively and spirited debate from Congress.
   b. could exercise power comparatively unfettered.
   c. acted upon concerns of public opinion.
   d. felt more comfortable with his expertise and talents.

9. For Theodore Roosevelt, the definition of a "civilized" nation seemed to depend largely upon its:
   a. ability and willingness to engage in physical combat.
   b. degree of economic development.
   c. historical and cultural accomplishments.
   d. adoption of the Christian religion.

10. The right of the United States to intervene in the domestic affairs of Latin American nations to maintain order was asserted in the:
    a. Monroe Doctrine.
    b. Roosevelt Corollary.
    c. Stimson Doctrine.
    d. Teller Amendment.

11. Which of the following Latin American and/or Caribbean nations were subjected to United States military intervention prior to 1917?
    a. Mexico and Cuba
    b. Nicaragua and Panama
    c. Haiti and the Dominican Republic
    d. All of the above

12. In Latin America, President Taft sought to:
    a. topple the regimes of military dictators.
    b. extend America's economic investments.
    c. remove all American military troops.
    d. join with European nations in railroad development.

13. The result of Wilson's military intervention in Mexico was:
    a. the capture and execution of Pancho Villa by Mexican authorities.
    b. the establishment of friendly relations with the new Carranza regime.
    c. the successful mediation of the dispute by an international commission.
    d. a lasting Mexican hostility toward the United States.

14. The site chosen for the Panama Canal lay within the boundaries of what country *before* a "revolution" created the nation of Panama?
    a. Colombia
    b. Nicaragua
    c. Costa Rica
    d. Guatemala

15. The naval force that Roosevelt sent on a world cruise to showcase U.S. strength was nicknamed the:
    a. Big Stick Flotilla.
    b. Bully Squadron.
    c. Yankee Armada.
    d. Great White Fleet.

True/False

Read each statement carefully. Mark true statements "T" and false statements "F."

___1. Theodore Roosevelt became president as a result of the assassination of William McKinley.

___2. As president, Roosevelt contended that big businesses or trusts were an unnatural occurrence in the economy and that the federal government had the obligation to "bust" them down to a more natural size.

___3. By offering to mediate a major coal strike, Roosevelt was moving to take the federal government away from an antilabor stance toward a more neutral approach.

___4. Roosevelt opposed the Pure Food and Drug Act and the Meat Inspection Acts because they interfered with the laissez-faire rights of business.

___5. The conservation movement was somewhat internally divided between those who stressed the preservation of natural resources and those who stressed managed exploitation of those resources.

___6. Roosevelt blamed the Panic of 1907 on bankers and financiers and refused to cooperate with them in any efforts to revive the economy.

___7. Roosevelt and William Howard Taft had been longtime rivals in the Republican Party before Taft became Roosevelt's vice president.

___8. In the period between the time he left the White House and the outbreak of World War I, Roosevelt drifted away from progressivism and became more and more conservative in his approach to national policy issues.

___9. Woodrow Wilson's so-called New Freedom program called for more effort to break up big business combinations than Roosevelt's New Nationalism did.

___10. Roosevelt's Progressive Party of 1912 was nicknamed the "Bull Moose" party.

___11. As president, Woodrow Wilson advocated a general lowering of the nation's tariff rates.

___12. The Federal Reserve Act made individual bank failures less likely but had little effect on the nation's basic circulating currency.

___13. Theodore Roosevelt believed that the United States should reduce its world commitments and concentrate instead on domestic reform.

___14. William Howard Taft's approach to foreign policy was given the nickname "Dollar Diplomacy."

___15. The United States militarily intervened in Mexican affairs during Woodrow Wilson's administration.

Review Questions

These questions are to be answered with essays. This will allow you to explore relationships among individuals, events, and attitudes of the period under review.

1. In what ways did Theodore Roosevelt transform the role of the presidency and the national government? What specific programs resulted from his vigorous executive leadership?

2. Were the differences between the Taft administration and those of Roosevelt and Wilson more a matter of beliefs and objectives or of personalities and leadership styles?

3. Considering Roosevelt's and Wilson's personalities and proposals, what would have happened to domestic reform and foreign relations if Roosevelt had won the Republican nomination in 1912 and become president again?

4. How did the Spanish-American War set the stage for America's Latin American policy in the early twentieth century?

CHAPTER TWENTY-THREE
America and the Great War

OBJECTIVES

A thorough study of Chapter 23 should enable you to understand:

1. The background factors and the immediate sequence of events that caused the United States to declare war on Germany in 1917.
2. The scale and nature of the fighting in World War I, including especially the impact of new technologies of warfare.
3. The contributions of the American military to Allied victory in World War I.
4. The extent of government control of the economy during World War I.
5. Propaganda and the extent of war hysteria in the United States during World War I.
6. The aspirations that the war raised with African Americans and how those hopes were dashed.
7. Woodrow Wilson's successes and failures at Versailles.
8. The circumstances that led the United States to reject the Treaty of Versailles.
9. The economic problems the United States faced immediately after the war.
10. The reasons for the Red Scare, and the resurgence of labor unrest in postwar America.

PERTINENT QUESTIONS

The Road to War (pp. 680–685)

1. How did World War I begin? What connections to conflicts in the 1990s are apparent?
2. Which nations were referred to as the Allies in World War I?
3. What forced President Woodrow Wilson out of his professed stance of true neutrality? To what degree was his decision based on economics?

4. Why did Germany rely on U-boats (submarines)? Why did it back off from the unrestricted use of U-boats early in the war?

5. Before 1917, how did Wilson balance the demands for preparedness and the cries for peace? What effect did his position have on the 1916 election?

6. What key events early in 1917 combined to finally bring the United States fully into World War I?

"War Without Stint" (pp. 686–695)

7. On what aspect of the war did American entry have the most immediate effect? What was the effect?

8. What impact did events in Russia have on the decision of the United States to enter World War I and on the need for American land forces in Europe after entry?

9. What role did American ground forces play in the conflict?

10. How did new technologies used in World War I such as airplanes, chemical weapons, and improved machine guns change the nature of warfare?

11. On what two methods did the Wilson administration depend to finance the war effort? How did the war cost compare with the typical peacetime budgets of that era?

12. Describe the role of the War Industries Board (WIB) and the National War Labor Board. How successful were they? What implications did they have for the future of American politics?

13. What tactics did the Committee on Public Information employ to propagandize the American people into unquestioning support of the war effort?

14. In what ways did the government use the Sedition Act and related legislation to suppress criticism? Who suffered most?

15. How did private acts of oppression supplement the official campaign to suppress diversity and promote unity? Who suffered most?

The Search for a New World Order (pp. 695–698)

16. Into what three major categories did the Fourteen Points fall?

17. What obstacles did Wilson face in getting the European leaders to accept his approach to peace? What domestic development weakened his position?

18. Despite President Wilson's disappointments at Versailles, what was his most visible triumph?

19. Who were the main domestic opponents of American entry into the League of Nations? What were the two categories of opponents? How much of the blame for the treaty's defeat must be laid on Wilson himself?

A Society in Turmoil (pp. 698–704)

20. What happened to the American economy in the postwar years? Why?
21. What inspired the labor unrest of 1919? What were the most important strikes? What did the wave of strikes reveal about the labor movement?
22. Describe how African-American military and industrial contributions during World War I raised black aspirations. How did whites react, and what happened after the war?
23. What led to the string of race riots during and shortly after the war? What were the riots like, and where was the worst episode?
24. What inspired the Red Scare of 1919 to 1920? Was the threat real or imagined?
25. What did the results of the election of 1920 indicate about the mood of the American people?

IDENTIFICATION

Identify each of the following, and explain why it is important within the context of the chapter.

1. Triple Entente/Triple Alliance
2. Archduke Franz Ferdinand
3. Ottoman Empire
4. *Lusitania*
5. Zimmermann telegram
6. V. I. Lenin
7. Bolshevik Revolution
8. American Expeditionary Force (AEF)
9. John J. Pershing
10. Argonne Forest campaign
11. mustard gas
12. "dogfights"
13. Liberty Bonds
14. Herbert Hoover
15. Bernard Baruch
16. Industrial Workers of the World (IWW)
17. Eugene V. Debs

18. David Lloyd George
19. Georges Clemenceau
20. Vittorio Orlando
21. Henry Cabot Lodge
22. "Great Migration"
23. Marcus Garvey
24. A. Mitchell Palmer
25. Sacco-Vanzetti case
26. "normalcy"

DOCUMENT

Read the text section entitled "A War for Democracy" (p. 684), paying careful attention to the discussion of the Zimmermann telegram. The following document is the official dispatch in which Walter Hines Page, the American ambassador to Great Britain, informed the State Department that the British had intercepted Germany's invitation to Mexico to join in war against the United States. Unknown to the Germans, the British had broken their diplomatic code. Read the dispatch, and consider the following questions: How did the Zimmermann communication combine with other events early in 1917 to impel the United States to declare war? Why did Germany have reason to believe that Mexico might be receptive to a proposal to wage war against the United States? Why did the British government give a copy of the Zimmermann note to the United States? How does Zimmermann's note reveal that Germany expected the United States to enter the war soon?

The Ambassador of Great Britain [Walter Hines Page] to the Secretary of State [Robert Lansing]

LONDON, February 24, 1917, 1 P.M.

[Received 8:30 P.M.]

. . . British Foreign Secretary Arthur] Balfour has handed me the text of a cipher telegram from [Arthur] Zimmermann, German Secretary of State for Foreign Affairs, to the German Minister to Mexico. . . . I give you the English translation as follows:

We intend to begin on the 1st of February unrestricted submarine warfare. We shall endeavor in spite of this to keep the United States of America neutral. In the event of this not succeeding, we make Mexico a proposal of alliance on the following basis: make war together, make peace together, generous financial support and an understanding on our part that Mexico is to reconquer the lost territory in Texas, New Mexico, and Arizona. The settlement in detail is left to you. You will inform the President [of Mexico, Venustiano Carranza] of the above most secretly as soon as the outbreak of war with the United States of America is certain and add the suggestion that he should, on his own initiative, invite Japan to immediate adherence and at the same time mediate between Japan and ourselves. Please call the President's attention to the fact that the

250

ruthless employment of our submarines now offers the prospect of compelling England in a few months to make peace.

Signed, Zimmermann.

The receipt of this information has so greatly exercised the British Government that they have lost no time in communicating it to me to transmit to you, in order that our Government may be able without delay to make such disposition as may be necessary in view of the threatened invasion of our territory. . . .

U.S. Department of State, *Papers Relating to the Foreign Relations of the U.S.,* 1917, Supplement 1, The World War (Washington, D.C.: Government Printing Office, 1931), p. 147.

MAP EXERCISE

Fill in or identify the following on the blank map provided.
1. The Allies, the Central Powers, the occupied nations, and the neutrals.
2. Paris, Berlin, London, and Vienna.
3. The principal area of submarine warfare.
4. Approximate location of Germany's deepest penetration of France.
5. Approximate location of Germany's deepest penetration of Russia.
6. Approximate location of the armistice line.

Interpretative Questions

Based on what you have filled in, answer the following. On some of the questions you will need to consult the narrative in your text for information or explanation.

1. What two nations bore the brunt of the western front fighting within their borders? What nation suffered the most on the east? How did this affect the peace negotiations?
2. Why was the ocean war so crucial in bringing the United States into the war?
3. What geographic and naval advantages did Great Britain have in sea warfare? How did Germany try to counter these advantages and how successful was it?

SUMMARY

Following two and a half years of pro-Allied "neutrality," the United States entered World War I because of economic and cultural factors as well as German submarine warfare. In the face of powerful new technologies such as mustard gas and machine guns that could put forth withering fire, the armies and civilians of Europe had already suffered mightily by the time the United States finally entered. American forces, initially at sea and then on land, provided the margin of victory for the Allies. To mount its total effort, the United States turned to an array of unprecedented measures: sharply graduated taxes, conscription for a foreign war, bureaucratic management of the economy, and a massive propaganda and antisedition campaign. The war effort at home and overseas seemed to offer new opportunities for black Americans, but most of their hopes were dashed after the war. President Woodrow Wilson formulated American war aims in his famous Fourteen Points, but he was unable to convince either Europe or the United States to fully accept them as the basis for peace. By 1920, the American people, tired from nearly three decades of turmoil, had repudiated Wilson's precious League of Nations in favor of an illusion called "normalcy."

CHAPTER SELF-TEST

After you have read the chapter in the text and done the exercises in the study guide, the following self-test can be taken to see if you understand the material you have covered. Answers appear at the end of the study guide.

Multiple Choice

Circle the letter of the response that best answers the question or completes the statement.

1. Americans responded to the outbreak of the Great War in 1914 with a conviction that the conflict:
   a. would be quickly and peacefully resolved.
   b. would remain a limited war.
   c. had little to do with them.
   d. required their immediate intervention.

2. Though the bulk of the intensive trench warfare of World War I occurred in Belgium and France, the events that triggered the war took place in:
   a. the Balkan region of Bosnia and Serbia.
   b. western Russia along the Polish border.
   c. northern Italy.
   d. Scandinavia.

3. President Wilson protested German violations of American neutrality more harshly than British violations because:
   a. he admired the British and instinctively favored their cause.
   b. a profitable trade was resulting between the United States and the Allies.
   c. German violations cost American lives.
   d. All of the above

4. In the Zimmermann telegram, Germany:
   a. notified the United States it would begin unrestricted submarine warfare on February 1, 1917.
   b. offered Russian revolutionists aid for a plot to overthrow the czarist regime.
   c. proposed to Mexico a military alliance in the event of war between Germany and the United States.
   d. offered aid to German Americans for plans of industrial sabotage.

5. After the Bolshevik Revolution in November, 1917, the new Russian government, led by V. I. Lenin:
   a. negotiated a hasty peace with the Central Powers.
   b. negotiated secret treaties with the Allied Powers to divide the postwar spoils.
   c. supplied the necessary troops that would guarantee Allied success.
   d. called for creation of a world government to maintain international peace and security.

6. Members of the American Expeditionary Force (AEF) played a crucial role in the fighting at:
   a. the Marne.
   b. Verdun.
   c. the Somme.
   d. the Argonne Forest.

7. In mobilizing the American economy for war, the War Industries Board:
   a. divided the country geographically, setting up local defense councils in each region.
   b. operated with incredible success and efficiency.
   c. worked to restrict private power and limit corporate profits.
   d. established a mutually beneficial alliance between government and the private sector.

8. During World War I, German Americans suffered all of the following forms of abuse *except:*
   a. a campaign to purge society of all things German.
   b. the loss of jobs.
   c. the loss of homes and internment in camps.
   d. physical harassment and beatings.

9. Woodrow Wilson's Fourteen Points:
   a. included specific formulas for the implementation of national self-determination.
   b. specifically addressed the needs of the new Soviet government in Russia.
   c. reflected his belief that the world as a whole was capable of just and efficient government.
   d. attracted the strong, enthusiastic support of the Allied leaders.

10. Wilson's most notable triumph at the Paris Peace Conference was the:
    a. impartial mediation and settlement of colonial claims.
    b. creation of a League of Nations.
    c. establishment of national self-determination for all Europeans.
    d. obstruction of demands for punitive damages from the defeated Central Powers.

11. Wilson's cross-country tour to arouse support for the Treaty of Versailles:
   a. generated enough enthusiasm and popular support to pressure the Senate into ratification.
   b. exhausted Wilson and precipitated a serious stroke.
   c. convinced Wilson to accept significant changes in the treaty's language.

12. During World War I and the aftermath, Herbert Hoover established a reputation as:
   a. a great military tactician and adviser.
   b. an efficient administrator and true humanitarian.
   c. a creative public relations expert and propagandist.
   d. an apologist for German aggression and atrocities.

13. Which of the following was *not* one of the three principal negotiators who joined Woodrow Wilson at the Versailles conference?
   a. David Lloyd George
   b. Vittorio Orlando
   c. Georges Clemenceau
   d. Bernard Baruch

14. The catch phrase used by Warren Harding in the 1920 campaign to communicate that the people wanted to put the turmoil of the war years behind them was:
   a. "search for stability."
   b. "return to normalcy."
   c. "seeking for security."
   d. "calling for calm."

15. The so-called Great Migration of World War I and the years before and after involved the movement of:
   a. Asian Americans from the West Coast to the rest of the nation.
   b. Hispanics from Mexico into the American Southwest.
   c. African Americans from the rural South to the urban North.
   d. poor white farmers to California.

True/False

Read each statement carefully. Mark true statements "T" and false statements "F."

___1.   For the first part of World War I, Russia was an ally of Great Britain and France.

___2.   At the time of its sinking by German submarine, the British ocean liner *Lusitania* was carrying munitions as well as passengers.

___3. Woodrow Wilson's victorious presidential campaign in 1916 was significantly aided by his pledge that the United States would enter World War I on the Allied side if he were reelected.

___4. The episode involving the intercepted telegram from Arthur Zimmermann concerned German relations with Mexico.

___5. Although German scientists had developed chemical weapons such as mustard gas, they refrained from employing them for fear that the Allies would retaliate with their own poison gas.

___6. The most immediate effect that the U.S. had on the war once it joined was at sea versus German U-boats.

___7. The biggest defeat of American ground forces in World War I was in the Argonne Forest.

___8. In order to keep support for the war high, the federal government chose to raise all extra funds by selling war bonds rather than raising taxes.

___9. As President Wilson's principal economic adviser during World War I, Bernard Baruch adopted a hands-off policy and let market forces determine wartime industrial output.

___10. Government actions during World War I resulted in a significant increase in labor union membership between 1917 and 1919.

___11. Unlike France and Great Britain, where opposition to the war was treated harshly, the United States allowed dissidents to speak and operate freely without supervision or harassment.

___12. A major category of Wilson's Fourteen Points concerned his aspirations for postwar European boundaries and self-determination for the people of the Austro-Hungarian and Ottoman Empires.

___13. Wilson's Fourteen Points contained proposals for an alliance of western European powers against the newly-created Soviet Union.

___14. When Wilson traveled to Paris for the peace conference, he visited several European cities and encountered considerable public hostility toward his idealistic ideas for peace.

___15. In the United States Senate the leader of the opposition to Wilson, the treaty, and the League of Nations was Henry Cabot Lodge.

Review Questions

These questions are to be answered with essays. This will allow you to explore relationships among individuals, events, and attitudes of the period under review.

1. Was American involvement in World War I inevitable? What forces worked to maintain neutrality? What forces propelled the country away from neutrality and into full belligerency?

2. Describe the suffering that the Great War visited on Europe. Why is it said that the United States emerged from the war as "the only real victor"?

3. Despite his tumultuous reception by the peoples of Europe and the generally favorable response he received on his tour in the western United States, Wilson faced troublesome opposition from both European statesmen and the United States senators. Why did he encounter such intransigence? Did he respond in a rational and politically effective way?

CHAPTER TWENTY-FOUR

The New Era

OBJECTIVES

A thorough study of Chapter 24 should enable you to understand:
1. The reasons for the industrial boom in the 1920s after the initial period of economic readjustment following World War I.
2. The nature and extent of labor's problems.
3. The plight of the American farmer.
4. The changes in the American way of life and American values in the 1920s in the areas of consumerism, communications, religion, and the role of women.
5. The effects of prohibition on American politics and society.
6. The reasons for xenophobia and racial unrest in the 1920s.
7. The debacle of the Harding administration.
8. The pro-business tendencies of the Republican administration in the 1920s.

PERTINENT QUESTIONS

The New Economy (pp. 706–713)

1. Outline the causes of the economic boom of the 1920s. What impact did the spectacular growth of the automobile industry have on related business activities?
2. How did the birth of commercial radio and the rapid spread of telephones alter everyday life in the 1920s?
3. What developments in the "New Era" laid the groundwork for future technological advances in radar, computers, and genetics?
4. What was the trend in business organization? What sort of firms were less likely to consolidate?
5. What were the elements of "welfare capitalism"? How much did the average worker truly benefit from welfare capitalism and the general prosperity of the decade?
6. To what extent was the lag in union membership due to the unions themselves? What were the other causal factors?

7. How did the African Americans, Hispanics, and Asians fare with labor unions?

8. What national group composed the largest number of immigrants in the 1920s? Where did they concentrate, and how were they treated?

9. What caused the big drop in farm prices and income in the 1920s? Explain how parity was designed to solve the problem. What happened to the parity concept?

The New Culture (pp. 714–720)

10. Describe the new urban consumer society. How did advertising help shape it?

11. How did newspaper chains, mass-circulation magazines, movies, and radio serve as unifying and nationalizing forces in America?

12. Compare and contrast Freudian psychology with behavioralism. How did these psychological views and the rise of medical psychiatry lead to changes in treatment for disorders and ordinary anxieties?

13. How did the image of the "new professional woman" compare with reality for most working women?

14. What new attitudes toward motherhood, sex, and leisure developed in the 1920s, especially among middle-class women? Was the new woman mostly a figure of myth?

15. What social forces combined to disenchant many intellectuals? What did these people attack? Who were the main attackers?

A Conflict of Cultures (pp. 720–725)

16. What more basic conflict in society did the controversy over the "noble experiment" of prohibition come to symbolize? What were the results of prohibition?

17. Explain the changes in immigration laws brought about by the National Origins Act and subsequent legislation. What ethnic groups were favored?

18. What helped resurrect the Ku Klux Klan? In addition to African Americans, at whom did the Klan target its rage? How influential was it?

19. Compare and contrast the views of the religious modernists and fundamentalists. How did Darwinism and the Scopes trial symbolize the conflict between the two? How has the conflict persisted?

20. How were the cultural tensions of the 1920s reflected in the Democratic Party?

21. What features of President Warren G. Harding's personal background led to his political repudiation? What was the biggest of the various Harding-era scandals?
22. Contrast the personal lives of Harding and Calvin Coolidge. Did their politics and policies differ as much as their personalities?
23. What approach did the Harding and Coolidge administrations take toward taxes and the federal budget?
24. What role did Herbert Hoover play before his presidency? What concept did he champion most vigorously?

INDENTIFICATION

Identify each of the following, and explain why it is important within the context of the chapter.

1. "normalcy"
2. "ham radio"
3. nylon
4. American Plan
5. "pink collar" jobs
6. A. Philip Randolph
7. Issei/Nisei
8. barrios
9. *The Man Nobody Knows*
10. KDKA
11. John Watson
12 Margaret Sanger
13 "flapper"
14. Equal Rights Amendment
15. H. L. Mencken
16. Sinclair Lewis
17. "Harlem Renaissance"
18. Langston Hughes
19. "wets" and "drys"
20. Leo Frank case
21. ACLU
22. Clarence Darrow/William Jennings Bryan
23. Alfred E. Smith
24. Andrew Mellon

DOCUMENT

Read H. L. Mencken's obituary for Calvin Coolidge, noting his contempt for politics and his sarcasm concerning Coolidge's lack of aggressiveness. Mencken's iconoclastic style was extremely popular with young intellectuals; but, in fact, his *American Mercury* was not a mass-circulation magazine, and Mencken's comments reached a relatively small portion of the general public. How did the public's view of President Coolidge differ from Mencken's acerbic view?

> In what manner he would have performed himself if the holy angels had shoved the Depression forward a couple of years—this we can only guess, and one man's hazard is as good as another's. My own is that he would have responded to bad times precisely as he responded to good ones—that is, by pulling down the blinds, stretching his legs upon his desk, and snoozing away the lazy afternoons. . . . He slept more than any other President, whether by day or by night. Nero fiddled, but Coolidge only snored. . . . Counting out Harding as a cipher only, Dr. Coolidge was preceded by one World Saver and followed by two more. What enlightened American, having to choose between any of them and another Coolidge, would hesitate for an instant? There were no thrills while he reigned, but neither were there any headaches. He had no ideas, and he was not a nuisance.

H. L. Mencken, *American Mercury,* April 1933.

MAP EXERCISE

Fill in or identify the following on the blank map provided. Use the maps in the text as your sources.

1. Locate and label the following cities: Boston, New York, Philadelphia, Chicago, Nashville, Atlanta, Birmingham, Memphis, Dallas–Fort Worth, Denver, Seattle, San Francisco, Los Angeles.
2. Circle the region of the nation that was most heavily urbanized as of 1920.
3. Shade in the states that Al Smith carried in the election of 1928.

Interpretative Questions

Based on what you have filled in, answer the following. For some of the questions you will need to consult the narrative in your text for information or explanation.

1. To what extent were the new consumerism and the change in communication related to increasing urbanization in the United States?

2. Why did Al Smith carry states in such different regions—the urban Northeast and the more rural South? Why did he not carry as much of the South as a Democrat of that period normally would have?

SUMMARY

Through the mid-1920s, America enjoyed unparalleled prosperity fueled by a great boom in automobiles, related businesses, and other new technologies such as the radio. Many people believed that the progressive ideal of an efficient, ordered society was at hand. The boom, however, masked problems. The prosperity was not equitably distributed through society; many workers and farmers were left out, and, as usual, racial and ethnic minorities were excluded from most economic benefits. The new ways forged by economic and technological advancement brought an unprecedented cultural nationalism, but they also aroused serious conflicts as both intellectuals and traditionalists attacked elements of the New Era culture. Presidents Harding and Coolidge, despite their contrasting styles, personified the pro-business policies of the Republican Party, which dominated American politics throughout the 1920s and culminated in the election of Herbert Hoover in 1928.

CHAPTER SELF-TEST

After you have read the chapter in the text and done the exercises in the study guide, the following self-test can be taken to see if you understand the material you have covered. Answers appear at the end of the study guide.

Multiple Choice

Circle the letter of the response that best answers the question or completes the statement.

1. America's economic boom in the 1920s resulted from the:
    a. debilitation of Europe after World War I.
    b. rapid pace of technological innovations.
    c. expansion of the automobile industry.
    d. All of the above

2. Which of the following was *not* an arena of technological advance in the 1920s?
    a. Analog computer
    b. Genetic research
    c. Synthetic fibers
    d. Satellites

3. Which of the following was *not* provided by the "welfare capitalism" of the 1920s?
    a. Wage and hours increases for some workers
    b. Company unions or workers, councils in many companies
    c. Significant control of the work environment by industrial employees
    d. Pensions for retirees of some corporations

4. Most American industrial workers in the 1920s:
    a. received wage increases that were proportionately below the increases in corporate profits.
    b. became increasingly militant and committed to unionization as the means for improving their position.
    c. experienced sufficient increases in their standard of living to place them in the middle class.

5. The plight of the American farmers in the 1920s resulted most directly from the:
   a. failure of agriculture to adapt to changing technology.
   b. depleted fertility of the land.
   c. inability of American agriculture to service an expanded European market.
   d. overproduction by American farmers.

6. In the 1920s, most working women in America:
   a. were college graduates.
   b. entered professional fields.
   c. attempted to combine marriage and careers.
   d. were employed in nonprofessional, low-paying jobs.

7. Many American artists and intellectuals of the 1920s felt alienated by modern American society for all of the following reasons *except* its:
   a. obsession with materialism.
   b. outmoded, straight-laced morality.
   c. lack of idealism.
   d. emphasis on individualism.

8. Immigration to the United States was restricted in the 1920s on the basis of:
   a. religion.
   b. national origin.
   c. special skills or talents.
   d. need for political asylum.

9. Which of the following characteristics did *not* apply to President Warren G. Harding?
   a. Good looks and geniality
   b. Polished speaking style
   c. Aggressive leadership
   d. Party regularity

10. Like Harding, Calvin Coolidge:
    a. was tolerant of corruption among his cronies.
    b. had a loose, debauched lifestyle.
    c. took a passive, conservative approach to the presidency.
    d. had been a major congressional leader before taking executive office.

11. As Commerce secretary for much of the 1920s, Herbert Hoover advocated:
    a. vigorous enforcement of antitrust legislation.
    b. voluntary business cooperation through trade associations.
    c. government-sanctioned collusion among manufacturers.
    d. the establishment of government relief programs.

12. Al Smith, Democratic presidential nominee in 1928, gained his strongest support at the party convention from:
    a. rural southern delegates.
    b. "dry" delegates from all regions.
    c. northeastern urban delegates.
    d. midwestern small-town delegates.

13. A method of mass commercial communication that was totally new to the 1920s was:
    a. popular magazines.
    b. radio.
    c. television.
    d. daily newspapers.

14. The revived Ku Klux Klan dedicated itself to:
    a. defending what it considered to be traditional values.
    b. promoting the ideal of racial integration.
    c. secularizing American society.
    d. helping southern European immigrants adapt to America.

15. The Scopes trial of 1925:
    a. illustrated the power of business corporations.
    b. personified intellectual alienation.
    c. symbolized religious conflict between fundamentalists and modernists.
    d. solidified the open-shop concept.

True/False

Read each statement carefully. Mark true statements "T" and false statements "F."

___1. The Democratic Party of the 1920s consisted of a diverse coalition of interests that often faced internal conflicts.

___2. The "American Plan" was a nickname given by corporate leaders to the "open shop" concept, which held that no worker could be required to join a union to get or keep a job.

___3. The economic sector most responsible for the prosperity of the 1920s was agriculture.

___4. Religious opposition to "tampering with God's creation" prevented any significant genetic research in America during the 1920s.

___5. During the 1920s, membership in labor unions declined significantly compared to the World War I years.

___6. The concept of "parity" for agricultural prices was designed to make sure that farmers earned at least the cost of producing the products.

___7. During the 1920s, advertising expanded rapidly and advertisers were increasingly trying to identify their products with a modern lifestyle.

___8. "Flapper" was the nickname given during the 1920s to middle-class women who "raised a flap" about the decline of traditional female roles and who criticized the "wild" ways of the youth of the decade.

___9. H. L. Mencken and Sinclair Lewis were among the authors whose writings were harshly critical of the dominant middle-class values of the 1920s.

___10. The New York City–based flourishing of African-American culture in the 1920s was nicknamed the "Gotham Revival."

___11. Although there were big city backers of prohibition, support for the prohibition of liquor was strongest in the provincial, largely rural, Protestant-dominated areas of the country.

___12. The effect of the Immigration Act of 1921 and the National Origins Act of 1924 was to increase foreign immigration, especially Asian immigration, following the restrictive period around World War I.

___13. In the 1920s, the Ku Klux Klan grew rapidly in some midwestern states as well as in the South.

___14. Within American Protestantism, the so-called modernists tended to be urban, middle-class people who attempted to adapt religion to the teachings of science and secular society.

___15. The Republican administrations of the 1920s achieved significant reductions in taxes on corporate profits, personal incomes, and inheritances.

Review Questions

These questions are to be answered with essays. This will allow you to explore relationships among individuals, events, and attitudes of the period under review.

1. Many people gained from the boom of the New Era, and others fell through the economic cracks. But the prosperity was

widespread enough to usher in a modern consumer society. Who gained? Who did not? What were the main elements of the national consumer-based society?

2. One of the questions that has troubled historians concerns the legacy of progressivism. Looking at the 1920s, would you say that progressive thought had died or had triumphed? Why?

3. Impressions of the 1920s vary, according to which vision one accepts—that of members of the ruling elite, such as Andrew Mellon and Herbert Hoover; of the disenchanted, such as H. L. Mencken; of evangelicals such as Billy Sunday; or of the blacks in the Harlem Renaissance. Briefly describe each of those visions, and tell how one or several capture the real significance of the decade.

CHAPTER TWENTY-FIVE

The Great Depression

OBJECTIVES

A thorough study of Chapter 25 should enable you to understand:
1. The relationship between the stock market crash and the subsequent Great Depression.
2. The causes of the Depression and the reasons for its severity.
3. The problems of unemployment and the inadequacy of relief.
4. The particular problems of farmers in the Dust Bowl.
5. The impact of the Depression on minorities.
6. The impact of the Depression on working women and the American family.
7. The reflection of the economic crisis in American culture.
8. President Herbert Hoover's policies for fighting the Depression.

PERTINENT QUESTIONS

The Coming of the Depression (pp. 731–738)

1. What caused the stock market boom to get so out of hand? What was the crash like?
2. Which two industries were most responsible for the New Era prosperity and hence substantially to blame for the Great Depression when they slumped? Why did these and other industries have trouble selling accumulated inventory?
3. What impact did international trade and debt factors have on the American economy? What role did U.S. tariff policy play?
4. What happened to the banking system early in the Depression? What role did the Federal Reserve System play?

The American People in Hard Times (pp. 738–744)

5. Describe the extent of unemployment nationally and especially in key industrial cities. How effective were local, state, and private relief agencies in meeting the ravages of widespread unemployment?

6. Compare and contrast the impact of the Great Depression on blacks, Hispanics, and Asians with its impact on whites. What demographic shifts occurred in this period?
7. What effect did the Depression have on the role of women in general and black women in particular?
8. How did American families adjust to the pressures of hard times?

The Depression and American Culture (pp. 744–753)

9. What impact did the Depression experience have on the traditional success ethic value of Americans?
10. How were the hard times reflected in intellectual art and literature? (See also #14.)
11. What role did radio play for Depression-era Americans?
12. What American values and interests were reflected in the popular motion pictures and novels of the 1930s?
13. How much allure did such radical movements as communism and socialism have for Americans in the 1930s? What was the "Popular Front" approach and why did it end?
14. How did artists and writers, especially those on the political left, shape public perceptions of the human effects of the Depression?

The Ordeal of Herbert Hoover (pp. 753–759)

15. What were Herbert Hoover's first approaches to combating the Depression? How effective were they?
16. What was Hoover's new approach to the Depression after mid-1931? What caused his shift in emphasis?
17. What impact did Hoover's handling of the veterans' Bonus March have on his popularity?
18. What made Franklin Roosevelt such an attractive presidential candidate for the Democrats? Why did he win the 1932 election?
19. How did Roosevelt react to Hoover's demands for policy pledges during the desperate winter of 1932–1933?

IDENTIFICATION

Identify each of the following, and explain why it is important within the context of the chapter.

1. Dow Jones Industrial Average
2. Hawley-Smoot Tariff
3. "monetary" interpretation/Keynesian interpretation
4. "Dust Bowl"

5. "Okies"
6. Scottsboro case
7. Chicanos
8. Dale Carnegie
9. Erskine Caldwell
10. Richard Wright
11. *Amos 'n Andy*
12. soap opera
13. Will Hays
14. Frank Capra
15. Walt Disney
16. *Gone with the Wind*
17. *Life*
18. Abraham Lincoln Brigade
19. Norman Thomas
20. John Steinbeck
21. "Hoovervilles"
22. Reconstruction Finance Corporation
23. Farmers' Holiday Association
24. interregnum

DOCUMENT

The years 1932 and 1933 were the hardest of the Great Depression. Even normally conservative, business-oriented *Fortune* magazine was convinced that extraordinary measures were necessary in the face of the collapse of existing relief agencies and the inadequacy of the $300 million Emergency Relief Act. The excerpt below is from *Fortune's* September 1932 issue. Consider the following questions: Why were existing relief programs so inadequate? Why is it especially significant that a business-minded publication like *Fortune* would, in the autumn of 1932, stress the magnitude of the crisis and the failure of the response? What do you suppose the writer meant by the statement "One does not talk architecture while the house is on fire. . ."?

> There can be no serious question of the failure of those methods. For the methods were never seriously capable of success. They were diffuse, unrelated, and unplanned. The theory was that private charitable organizations and semi-public welfare groups, established to care for the old and the sick and the indigent, were capable of caring for the casualties of a worldwide economic disaster. And the theory in application meant that social agencies manned for the service of a few hundred families, and city shelters set up to house and feed a handful of homeless men, were compelled by the brutal necessities of hunger to care for hundreds of thousands of families and whole armies of the displaced and the jobless. And to depend for their

resources upon the contributions of communities no longer able to contribute, and upon the irresolution and vacillation of state legislatures and municipal assemblies long since in the red on their annual budgets. The result was the picture now presented in city after city and state after state—heterogeneous groups of official and semiofficial and nonofficial relief agencies struggling under the earnest and untrained leadership of the local men of affairs against an inertia of misery and suffering and want they are powerless to overcome. . . .

One does not talk architecture while the house is on fire and the tenants are still inside. The question at this moment is the pure question of fact. Having decided at last to face reality and do something about it, what is reality? How many men are unemployed in the U.S.? How many are in want? *What are the facts?*

The following minimal statements may be accepted as true—with the certainty that they underestimate the real situation:

1. Unemployment has steadily increased in the U.S. since the beginning of the depression and the rate of increase during the first part of 1932 was more rapid than in any other depression year.

2. The number of persons totally unemployed is now at least 10 million.

3. The number of persons totally unemployed next winter will, at the present rate of increase, be 11 million.

4. Eleven million unemployed means better than one man out of every four employable workers.

5. This percentage is higher than the percentage of unemployed British workers registered under the compulsory insurance laws (17.1 percent in May 1932, as against 17.3 percent in April and 18.4 percent in Jan.) and higher than the French, the Italian, and the Canadian percentages, but lower than the German (43.9 percent of trade unionists in April 1932) and the Norwegian.

6. Eleven million unemployed means 27,500,000 whose regular source of livelihood has been cut off.

7. Twenty-seven and a half million without regular income includes the families of totally unemployed workers alone. Taking account of the numbers of workers on part time, the total of those without adequate income becomes 34 million, or better than a quarter of the entire population of the country.

8. Thirty-four million persons without adequate income does not mean 34 million in present want. Many families have savings. But savings are eventually dissipated and the number in actual want tends to approximate the number without adequate income. How nearly it approximates it now or will next winter no man can say. But it is conservative to estimate that the problem of next winter's relief is a problem of caring for approximately 25 million souls . . . .

Such, broadly speaking, are the facts of unemployment relief in the late summer of 1932. Ahead, whether the depression "ends" this fall or not, is the problem of caring for some 25 million souls through what may prove to be one of the most difficult winters of the republic's history. Behind are three years of muddled purpose, insufficient funds, and unscientific funds, and unscientific direction. Across the threshold lies a new federal policy and a formal acceptance of the issue.

Fortune, September 1932.

MAP EXERCISE

Fill in or identify the following on the blank map provided. Use the map
on page 758 of the text as your source.
1. States carried by Hoover in the 1932 presidential election,
2. States carried by Roosevelt,

Interpretative Questions

Based on what you have filled in, answer the following. For some of the
questions you will need to consult the narrative in your text for
information or explanation.
1. Why did the nation so thoroughly reject Herbert Hoover? What
    was expected from Roosevelt?
2. What parts of the country that were normally reliably Republican
    voted for Roosevelt in 1932? What does that signify about the
    seriousness of the Depression?

SUMMARY

In October 1929, the stock market's overinflated values collapsed, and
the Great Depression began. Its causes were complex, and its
consequences were enormous. In a few short years, the 2 percent
unemployment rate of the 1920s had become the 25 percent rate of 1932.

The nation's political institutions were not equipped to respond. The task overwhelmed local and private relief efforts. President Herbert Hoover's tentative program of voluntary cooperation, big-business loans, and limited public works was activist by old standards but inadequate to the challenge. American tariffs and war-debt policy aggravated international economic problems and thereby added to domestic woes. Although the suffering of Americans, especially blacks, Asians, and Hispanics, was great, most citizens clung to traditional values and resisted radical solutions. With veterans marching, farmers protesting, and millions not working, Franklin Delano Roosevelt won the presidency.

CHAPTER SELF-TEST

After you have read the chapter in the text and done the exercises in the study guide, the following self-test can be taken to see if you understand the material you have covered. Answers appear at the end of the study guide.

Multiple Choice

Circle the letter of the response that best answers the question or completes the statement.

1. The stock market boom of the late 1920s rested primarily upon the:
   a. maintenance of high interest rates by stockbrokers.
   b. widespread speculative mania of American investors.
   c. increased earning power of American corporations.
   d. economic support of J. P. Morgan and Company.

2. There was a serious lack of diversification in the American economy of the 1920s, with prosperity excessively dependent upon what two industries?
   a. Oil and steel
   b. Railroads and public utilities
   c. Radio and motion pictures
   d. Construction and automobiles

3. The profits generated by America's economic expansion in the 1920s:
   a. went disproportionately to producers rather than potential consumers.
   b. lifted a great majority of the families in America above a minimum subsistence level.
   c. created a consistently expanding market for consumer goods.
   d. led corporations to neglect the expansion of capital facilities.

4. American banks of the 1920s:
   a. had most of their assets in agricultural land.
   b. protested tight regulations of the Federal Reserve System.
   c. invested wisely in the stock market.
   d. often made unwise loans and failed to maintain adequate reserves.

5. The international credit structure collapsed by the early 1930s to a great extent because:
   a. Germany defaulted on reparations payments it owed to the United States.
   b. the United States forgave the debts of the Allied Powers.
   c. high American tariffs restricted Europeans' ability to repay their loans.
   d. European demand for American goods increased too rapidly.

6. The Keynesian explanation for the Great Depression emphasized
   a. a drop in investment and consumer spending calling for government spending to counter the crisis.
   b. a lack of business confidence because corporate leaders feared government regulations and high taxes.
   c. the collapse of the international economy and credit structure beyond U.S. control.
   d. the contraction in the supply of currency caused by bad Federal Reserve Board decisions.

7. The industrial cities of the Northeast and Midwest in the early 1930s:
   a. largely escaped the high rates of unemployment burdening the nation as a whole.
   b. lacked sufficient resources and understanding to provide the necessary relief for unemployed workers.
   c. combined the efforts of private charities and local public relief systems to ensure adequate food and housing for all unemployed workers.
   d. convinced state governments of the need for establishment of a permanent welfare system.

8. American farmers faced all of the following problems during the 1930s *except:*
   a. an inability to produce enough food to feed Americans.
   b. one of the worst droughts in the history of the nation.
   c. a steady loss of land through mortgage foreclosures or evictions.
   d. creation of a Dust Bowl in a large area of the South and Midwest.

9. For black Americans, the Depression:
   a. actually reduced the average income gap between white and black families.
   b. mitigated white attitudes of racism and discrimination.
   c. weakened their commitment to and drive for economic and political equality.
   d. intensified problems and created special hardships.

10. The most effective documentation of rural poverty in the 1930s came from:
    a. fact-finding commissions of the national government.
    b. documentary photographers and perceptive novelists.
    c. the powerful instruments of popular culture—radio and the movies.
    d. the academic fields of sociology and anthropology.

11. Thousands of disillusioned members left the American Communist Party as a result of the:
    a. formation of the Abraham Lincoln Brigade for intervention in the Spanish Civil War.
    b. signing of a nonaggression pact in 1939 between the Soviet Union and Nazi Germany, and the end of the Popular Front approach.
    c. party's defense of extreme and violent tactics to achieve racial justice.
    d. party's refusal to engage actively in the organization and promotion of unions.

12. In response to the Depression, President Herbert Hoover called for a program of:
    a. voluntary cooperation among leaders of business, labor, and agriculture.
    b. massive and permanent federal public works projects.
    c. substantial government cutbacks to ensure a balanced budget.
    d. tax increases and tariff reductions.

13. The Hawley-Smoot Tariff of 1930:
    a. put tariff rates completely in the hands of the presidentially appointed Tariff Commission.
    b. provoked foreign governments to enact trade restrictions of their own in reprisal.
    c. helped expand the market for American agricultural goods.
    d. rendered industrial products more affordable to American farmers.

14. Hoover's use of the United States Army to clear the "Bonus Army" out of Washington, D.C.:
    a. increased congressional support for the immediate payment of a bonus to veterans of World War I.
    b. enhanced his reputation as a defender of law and order.
    c. confirmed his image as aloof and insensitive to the distress around him.
    d. offered proof of the growing and dangerous threat of radicalism in America.

15. Immediately prior to becoming President, Franklin D. Roosevelt served as:
    a. a U.S. Senator from Iowa, well known for holding hearings on problems in the banking industry.
    b. Secretary of State, well known for leading the isolationist movement.
    c. Speaker of the U.S. House of Representatives, well known for supporting organized labor.
    d. Governor of New York, well known for a positive program of government assistance early in the Depression.

True/False

Read each statement carefully. Mark true statements "T" and false statements "F."

___1. The stock market reached its lowest point of the Depression era in late 1929 and then gradually inched back up, finally reaching 1928 levels by mid-1932.

___2. Many economic historians contend that one important cause of the Great Depression was that the economy lacked diversification and too much of the prosperity had depended on automobiles and construction.

___3. Most economic historians believe that one important cause of the Great Depression was the U.S. decision early in the 1920s to forgive the debts that France and Great Britain owed to U.S. banks for loans taken out during World War I.

___4. In 1932, during the presidential campaign, unemployment in the United States stood at about 10 percent.

___5. Thousands of "Okies" and other families from the "Dust Bowl" region migrated to California in the 1930s.

___6. During the Great Depression several hundred thousand African Americans left the South to try to find better times in the industrial cities of the North.

___7. In general, the economic crisis of the Great Depression gave strength to the idea, if not the practice, that a woman should not hold a job outside the home if her husband was employed.

___8. Black women in the South suffered massive unemployment because many families cut back on domestic help during the Great Depression.

___9. In general, American social values apparently changed relatively little in response to the Depression. Rather, many people responded to hard times by redoubling their commitment to familiar success-focused ideas and goals.

___10. From 1935 through 1938, the American Communist Party adopted a "Popular Front" strategy that called for cooperation with other antifascist groups.

___11. President Herbert Hoover's first response to the Great Depression was to issue optimistic statements and meet with business leaders in an attempt to restore public confidence in the economy.

___12. President Hoover tried to help American farmers by raising tariffs on agricultural products from foreign farms.

___13. The Reconstruction Finance Corporation (RFC) was used by Hoover to create massive numbers of government-funded "make work" jobs for the unemployed.

___14. President Hoover's sagging popularity revived significantly in response to his support of the demands of the so-called Bonus Army.

___15. Franklin Roosevelt and Herbert Hoover worked cooperatively between the November 1932 election and the March 1933 nomination to assure the business community that the new president would not depart from economic orthodoxy.

Review Questions

These questions are to be answered with essays. This will allow you to explore relationships among individuals, events, and attitudes of the period under review.

1. List and explain the five factors that the text identifies as having been principally responsible for causing the Great Depression and making it so severe. How does the text's presentation fit with the varying interpretations that historians have advanced as discussed in "Debating the Past" (p. 735)?

2. On what causes of the Great Depression did Herbert Hoover place emphasis? How did that shape his response?

3. What did the Depression mean to typical Americans in terms of standard of living and lifestyle? What groups suffered especially? Why? How did basic American social, cultural, and political values stand up to the economic crisis?

CHAPTER TWENTY-SIX

The New Deal

OBJECTIVES

A thorough study of Chapter 26 should enable you to understand:

1. The series of emergency measures designed to restore confidence that were enacted during the early part of the New Deal.
2. The New Deal programs for raising farm prices and promoting industrial recovery.
3. The first federal efforts at regional planning.
4. The New Deal program for reforming the financial system.
5. The federal relief programs and Social Security.
6. The political pressures from both the left and the right that caused Franklin Roosevelt to move in new directions from 1935 on.
7. The changes in organized labor during the New Deal period.
8. The effects of the Court-packing scheme, and the recession of 1937 and 1938, on Roosevelt and the New Deal.
9. The impact of the New Deal on minorities and women.
10. The lasting significance of the New Deal to the American economy and political system.

PERTINENT QUESTIONS

Launching the New Deal (pp. 761–771)

1. What sort of relationship did President Roosevelt develop with the press and the public?
2. Why was banking the new president's number-one order of business? What was done immediately and later in the New Deal?
3. What did the Economy Act of 1933 reveal about Roosevelt's fundamental economic philosophy?
4. What measures were taken to restore confidence in the stock market?

5. What was the principal feature of New Deal farm policy? How well did it work? Which farmers were served best? Who was left out?

6. Describe the goals and concepts of the National Recovery Administration (NRA). Why was it less than fully successful? How did it end?

7. What were the goals and concepts of the Tennessee Valley Authority (TVA)? How well did it meet them?

8. What assumptions and values underlay the early relief programs of the Federal Emergency Relief Administration (FERA) and the Civil Works Administration (CWA)? What different dimension did the Civilian Conservation Corps (CCC) add?

The New Deal in Transition (pp. 772–781)

9. What organization led the conservative attack on Roosevelt in 1934 and 1935? Who were its main supporters?

10. How successful were the socialists and communists in exploiting the unrest caused by the Depression?

11. Briefly characterize the ideas of Huey Long, Francis Townsend, and Charles E. Coughlin. Who was probably most important among them? How did Roosevelt respond?

12. What 1935 legislative initiatives signaled the emergence of the Second New Deal? To what extent were these acts reactions to political agitation and court rulings?

13. Compare and contrast craft unionism and industrial unionism. What caused the split between the AFL and the CIO?

14. Why did organized labor become more militant in the 1930s? How did the Wagner Act help? In what industries did unions make especially significant gains?

15. What distinct programs other than the old-age pension system suported by payroll taxes, were provided for in the Social Security Act of 1935? What aspects of "insurance" rather than "welfare" were represented?

16. Describe the Works Progress Administration (WPA) and its accomplishments. How did it go beyond traditional public-works programs?

17. What were the elements of the New Deal–Democratic political coalition that propelled Roosevelt to victory in 1936?

The New Deal in Disarray (pp.781–783)

18. What was Roosevelt's objective in the "Court-packing" plan? What were the political repercussions of the episode?

19. What seems to have been the main cause of the 1937 recession? What economic notion appeared to be supported by the recession and the administration's response to it?

Limits and Legacies of the New Deal (pp. 784–788)

20. What did the New Deal offer to African Americans? What role did Eleanor Roosevelt play? What were the political implications of the New Deal approach?
21. What new direction in Indian policy did the Roosevelt administration take? What were the results of the new policy?
22. Describe how the New Deal represented a "breakthrough" in the role of women in public life. What cultural norms limited the opportunities for women?
23. Describe the impact the New Deal had on the West. Why was it greater than on other sections of the nation?

IDENTIFICATION

Identify each of the following, and explain why it is important within the context of the chapter.
1. "fireside chats"
2. "bank holiday"
3. Twenty-first Amendment
4. Harry Hopkins
5. Robert E. Wagner
6. John L. Lewis
7. sit-down strike
8. Frances Perkins
9. Alf M. Landon
10. Union Party
11. Fair Labor Standards Act
12. Mary McLeod Bethune
13. "Black Cabinet"
14. Indian Reorganization Act
15. Grand Coulee Dam

The New Deal created many "alphabet agencies," several of which still exist today. Explain the purpose of each of the following.
1. Federal Deposit Insurance Corporation (FDIC)
2. Securities and Exchange Commission (SEC)
3. Agricultural Adjustment Administration (AAA)
4. Rural Electrification Administration (REA)

5. National Recovery Administration (NRA)
6. Public Works Administration (PWA)
7. Tennessee Valley Authority (TVA)
8. Civilian Conservation Corps (CCC)
9. National Labor Relations Board (NLRB)
10. Works Progress Administration (WPA)

DOCUMENT

In the campaign of 1932, Franklin Roosevelt revealed little of what would become the New Deal. And during the interregnum of 1932 and 1933, he refused to announce the specifics of his program. In fact, some of his campaign speeches were so conservative that New Dealer Marriner Eccles later commented that they sometimes "read like a giant misprint in which Roosevelt and Hoover speak each other's lines." By March 1933, however, although he may not yet have known where he was headed, Roosevelt knew where he was going to start. The most quoted line of his first inaugural address was his famous dictum, "the only thing we have to fear is fear itself." The following excerpts are from later in the speech where he acknowledged the severity of the crisis and outlined his proposed course of action. Read the selection, and consider the following questions: How were Roosevelt's experiences as a member of the wartime Wilson administration reflected in his approach to the Depression? What values of the progressive era did the Roosevelt program embody? How many of the promised programs were implemented during the first two years of the New Deal? How many worked as intended?

> In such a spirit on my part and on yours, we face our common difficulties. They concern, thank God, only material things. Values have shrunken to fantastic levels; taxes have risen; our ability to pay has fallen; government of all kinds is faced by serious curtailment of income; the means of exchange are frozen in the currents of trade; the withered leaves of industrial enterprise lie on every side; farmers find no market for their produce; the savings of many years in thousands of families are gone.

> More important, a host of unemployed citizens face the grim problem of existence, and an equally great number toil with little return. Only a foolish optimist can deny the dark realities of the moment. . . .

> There must be an end to a conduct in banking and in business which too often has given to a sacred trust the likeness of callous and selfish wrongdoing.

> Small wonder that confidence languishes, for it thrives only on honesty, on honor, on the sacredness of obligations, on faithful protection, on unselfish performance; without them it cannot live.

> Restoration calls, however, not for changes in ethics alone. This nation asks for action, and action now.

Our greatest primary task is to put people to work. This is no unsolvable problem if we face it wisely and courageously.

It can be accomplished in part by direct recruiting by the government itself, treating the task as we would treat the emergency of a war, but at the same time, through this employment, accomplishing greatly needed projects to stimulate and reorganize the use of our natural resources.

Hand in hand with this, we must frankly recognize the overbalance of population in our industrial centers and, by engaging on a national scale in a redistribution, endeavor to provide a better use of the land for those best fitted for the land.

The task can be helped by definite efforts to raise the values of agricultural products and with this the power to purchase the output of our cities.

It can be helped by preventing realistically the tragedy of the growing loss, through foreclosure, of our small homes and our farms.

It can be helped by insistence that the Federal, State and local governments act forthwith on the demand that their cost be drastically reduced.

It can be helped by the unifying of relief activities which today are often scattered, uneconomical and unequal. It can be helped by national planning for and supervision of all forms of transportation and of communication and other utilities which have a definitely public character.

There are many ways in which it can be helped, but it can never be helped merely by talking about it. We must act, and act quickly.

Finally, in our progress toward a resumption of work we require two safeguards against a return of the evils of the old order; there must be a strict supervision of all banking and credits and investments; there must be an end to speculation with other people's money, and there must be provision for an adequate but sound currency.

MAP EXERCISE

Fill in or identify the following on the blank map provided. Use the narrative in the text and the maps in the back of the text as your sources.

1. Approximate route of the Tennessee River from its source to the Ohio River.
2. Note the states affected by the Tennessee River and its smaller tributaries not shown on the map.

Interpretative Questions

Based on what you have filled in, answer the following. For some of the questions you will need to consult the narrative in your text for information or explanation.

1. What development in the utility industry sparked the final approval of the TVA concept? What impact did the TVA have on the industry?
2. How did the TVA benefit the region? What were its limitations?
3. Why did the New Deal fail to embark on any other regional projects of the magnitude of the TVA?

SUMMARY

Franklin D. Roosevelt was bound by traditional economic ideas; but unlike Herbert Hoover, Roosevelt was willing to experiment and was able to show compassion. During the first two years of his New Deal, the groundwork was laid for a new relationship between government and the economy. Roosevelt sought temporary relief for the desperate unemployment plus long-term recovery and reform for industry and finance. Not everything worked, and the Depression was not stopped, but Roosevelt got the country moving again. In 1935, frustrated and facing pressures from all sides, Roosevelt launched a new set of programs, which sometimes is called the Second New Deal. The new programs were less conciliatory to big business and more favorable to the needs of workers and consumers than were those of the New Deal of 1933. Roosevelt was swept to reelection in 1936 by a new coalition of workers, blacks, and liberals. Soon, however, Roosevelt's political blunders in the Supreme Court fight and congressional purge effort combined with growing conservative opposition to halt virtually all New Deal momentum. The legacy of the New Deal was a more activist national government poised to serve as the broker among society's various interests.

CHAPTER SELF-TEST

After you have read the chapter in the text and done the exercises in the study guide, the following self-test can be taken to see if you understand the material you have covered. Answers appear at the end of the study guide.

Multiple Choice

Circle the letter of the response that best answers the question or completes the statement.

1. The New Deal resulted in all of the following *except* the:
   a. beginnings of a modern welfare system.
   b. extension of federal regulation over new areas of the economy.
   c. birth of the modern labor movement.
   d. full end of the Great Depression.

2. Much of Roosevelt's success in restoring public confidence in government can well be attributed to his:
   a. consistent application of clear-cut philosophies to social and economic problems.
   b. optimistic and ebullient personality.
   c. refusal to engage in press conferences.
   d. explicit public demonstration of how a man could overcome physical paralysis.

3. Roosevelt's most immediate concern as president was the:
   a. public panic caused by the bank failures.
   b. collapse of agriculture.
   c. problem of widespread unemployment.
   d. deflationary spiral that had crippled business.

4. The Twenty-first Amendment, ratified in 1933, repealed the:
   a. progressive income tax.
   b. poll tax, literacy test, and other discriminatory voting restrictions.
   c. prohibition of the manufacture and sale of alcoholic beverages.
   d. "quota system" of immigration limitations.
5. The basic goal of the Agricultural Adjustment Administration (AAA) and the Social conservation and Domestic Allotment Act was to improve the life of farmers by
   a. providing roads and electricity to rural areas.
   b. limiting production in order to raise prices.
   c. breaking up large landholdings and distributing land to former tenants and sharecroppers.
   d. reducing erosion and nutrient depletion.
6. Which of the following provisions was *not* included in the National Industrial Recovery Act of 1933?
   a. Trade association agreements on pricing and production
   b. Loans by the national government to railroads, banks, and insurance companies
   c. Legal protection to the right of workers to form unions and engage in collective bargaining
   d. A major program of public works
7. The Supreme Court declared the National Industrial Recovery Act unconstitutional because it:
   a. improperly delegated legislative power to the president and interfered with intrastate commerce.
   b. favored big business and encouraged monopoly.
   c. raised prices excessively while suppressing wage increases.
   d. allowed poorly written codes without adequate means of administration or enforcement.
8. The Tennessee Valley Authority (TVA):
   a. received strong support from the nation's utility companies.
   b. suffered as a result of the collapse of the electrical utility empire of Samuel Insull.
   c. was intended to serve as an agent for comprehensive redevelopment of the entire region.
   d. converted the Tennessee Valley into one of the most prosperous regions of the country.

9. The Roosevelt administration instituted all of the following financial actions and reforms *except*:
   a. inspection of banks before their reopening after the "bank holiday."
   b. establishment of the Federal Deposit Insurance Corporation (FDIC).
   c. transfer of control over interest rates from the Federal Reserve Board to Congress.
   d. establishment of the Securities and Exchange Commission (SEC) to police the stock market.

10. The right-wing group funded by wealthy industrialists to oppose Roosevelt and the New Deal was called:
    a. Share our Wealth.
    b. the Association for Economic Stability.
    c. the American Liberty League.
    d. the National Policy Foundation.

11. According to the flamboyant Louisiana politician Huey Long, the national government could end the Depression by:
    a. providing federal pensions for the elderly.
    b. taking actions to remonetize silver, issue additional greenbacks, and nationalize the banking system.
    c. ending its "dictatorial" policies and attacks on free enterprise.
    d. taxing the rich and sharing the wealth with others through income redistribution.

12. The National Labor Relations Act of 1935 sponsored by Senator Robert F. Wagner of New York:
    a. specifically outlawed "unfair practices" by which employers had fought unionization.
    b. offered fewer protections than had been provided by Section 7(a) of the National Industrial Recovery Act.
    c. was enthusiastically supported by President Roosevelt from the beginning of consideration.
    d. was declared unconstitutional by the Supreme Court on the grounds that only Congress could regulate interstate commerce.

13. A significant social development of the 1930s due to a great extent to action by the national government was:
    a. the elimination of legally enforceable racial discrimination and segregation in jobs and housing.
    b. the emergence of the powerful American trade union movement.
    c. the creation of a movement dedicated to the expansion of women's rights.
    d. an increasing rate of marriage and a subsequent "baby boom."

14. The Congress of Industrial Organization (CIO) had the intent of:
    a. organizing workers into a given union on the basis of their specific skill regardless of the worker's industry—e.g., welders.
    b. organizing workers into a given union on the basis of the specific industry in which they worked regardless of the worker's skill— e.g., automobile workers.
    c. converting factories into "profit-sharing" cooperative enterprises.
    d. eliminating the older, more conservative American Federation of Labor (AFL).

15. The United Auto Workers (UAW) gained union recognition from General Motors in 1937 after:
    a. staging a series of controversial but successful sit-down strikes.
    b. winning public sympathy following the brutal "Memorial Day Massacre" of peaceful demonstrators by police.
    c. gaining a federal court order to force company recognition.
    d. the company decided to relent rather than risk a costly strike at a time of economic recovery.

True/False

Read each statement carefully. Mark true statements "T" and false statements "F."

___1. President Franklin D. Roosevelt held frequent informal press conferences and won the respect and admiration of most reporters.

___2. The area of the economy that President Roosevelt first concentrated on was banking.

___3. The principal feature of New Deal agricultural policy was that it provided direct income supplements to farmers rather than trying to increase prices and thereby indirectly raise farm income.

___4. The Agricultural Adjustment Act turned out to be more beneficial to sharecroppers and tenant farmers than it was to landowning farmers.

___5. The basic idea of the National Recovery Administration (NRA) was that in exchange for the federal government's relaxing of antitrust laws, corporations would make concessions such as recognizing the right of workers to organize unions and establishing a minimum wage.

___6. The U.S. Supreme Court ruled the legislation creating the NRA void because Congress had unconstitutionally delegated legislative power to the president.

___7. The series of dams and related facilities built by the Tennessee Valley Authority virtually eliminated flooding in the region and brought electricity to thousands of people who had not had it before.

___8. The New Deal tried to revive the lagging stock market by removing the regulatory restrictions that had hampered brokers in the 1920s.

___9. The Civilian Conservation Corps, which housed young men in semimilitary camps and put them to work on such projects as tree planting and park development, was President Roosevelt's favorite relief program.

___10. President Roosevelt's supporters organized the "Liberty League" to counter those who argued that Roosevelt was moving the nation toward socialism.

___11. Senator Huey P. Long of Louisiana gathered a national following by arguing that a massive, across-the-board tax cut would rapidly stimulate the economy and end the Depression faster than the spending programs that Roosevelt advocated.

___12. In the so-called Second New Deal beginning in 1935, President Roosevelt's proposals were generally more conservative in an attempt to placate big business.

___13. The concept of "industrial unionism" is that all the workers in a particular industry, (e.g., automobiles), should belong to one union rather than joining specific craft unions (e.g., welders).

___14. The Works Progress Administration (WPA) not only provided work for traditional manual laborers, it also provided government-supported jobs for intellectual and creative workers such as writers, artists, musicians, and actors.

___15. As a consequence of the New Deal, the allegiance of most African-American voters switched from the Republican Party to the Democratic Party.

Review Questions

These questions are to be answered with essays. This will allow you to explore relationships among individuals, events, and attitudes of the period under review.

1. Which of Roosevelt's early New Deal programs illustrate his willingness to experiment with bold, innovative ideas? Which of his actions show his hesitation and attachment to conventional values?

2. What forces caused Roosevelt to launch his so-called Second New Deal programs in 1935? How did he steal the thunder from some of his most vocal opponents?

3. Compare the impact of the Depression on blacks, Hispanics, and Native Americans with its consequences for the typical white American.

4. What specific programs and general attitudes formed the important economic and political legacy of the New Deal?

5. Drawing from the "Debating the Past" section on p. 770, explain how many historians came to conclude that the "modern idea of New Deal liberalism bears only a limited relationship to the ideas that the New Dealers themselves embraced."

CHAPTER TWENTY-SEVEN

The Global Crisis, 1921–1941

OBJECTIVES

A thorough study of Chapter 27 should enable you to understand:

1. The new directions of American foreign policy in the 1920s.
2. The effects of the Great Depression on foreign relations.
3. The pattern of Japanese, Italian, and German aggression that eventually led to World War II.
4. The factors that led to the passage of neutrality legislation in the 1930s.
5. The specific sequence of events that brought the United States into the war.

PERTINENT QUESTIONS

The Diplomacy of the New Era (pp. 792–796)

1. What was accomplished by the Washington Conference?
2. Describe the circular pattern of international finance established by the Dawes Plan. What was the result?
3. How did President Hoover reshape U.S policy toward Latin America?
4. How did the Hoover administration deal with Japanese expansionism?

Isolationism and Internationalism (pp. 797–801)

5. How did Roosevelt break with Hoover on the matter of economic relations with Europe?
6. In what ways did the Good Neighbor policy of Roosevelt build on Hoover's Latin American policy?
7. What ideas and developments fed isolationist sentiment in the first half of the 1930s? What was Roosevelt's position?
8. Taken as a whole, what were the basic provisions and central purpose of the Neutrality Acts of 1935, 1936, and 1937?

9. How did President Roosevelt's stance toward the Spanish-American War and Japanese actions in China illustrate the strength of isolationist sentiment?
10. What German moves and diplomatic failures led to the start of World War II in Europe? What role did the Soviet Union play in the road to war?

From Neutrality to Intervention (pp. 801–806)

11. How did Roosevelt manage to aid Great Britain in 1939 and 1940 in various ways such as modifying the "cash and carry" principle, transferring destroyers, and establishing "lend-lease"?
12. What naval warfare developments led the United States to the brink of war in Europe?
13. What events in Asia brought Japan into conflict with the United States?
14. Why could the attack on Pearl Harbor be considered a tactical victory but a political blunder by the Japanese?

IDENTIFICATION

Identify each of the following, and explain why it is important within the context of the chapter.
1. Henry Cabot Lodge
2. isolationism
3. Charles Evans Hughes
4. Kellog-Briand Pact
5. Benito Mussolini
6. National Socialist (Nazi) Party
7. Aryan people
8. Chiang Kai-shek
9. diplomatic relations with the Soviet Union
10. World Court
11. Francisco Franco
12. *Panay* incident
13. "appeasement"
14. *blitzkrieg*
15. Vichy regime
16. America First Committee
17. Henry A. Wallace
18. Wendell Willkie
19. Atlantic Charter
20. Hideki Tojo

DOCUMENT

Read the text section entitled "The Rise of Isolationism" (p. 798), paying careful attention to the discussion of the investigations chaired by Senator Gerald P. Nye (R-N.D.). The following statements were made in May 1935 by Nye and Senator Bennett Champ Clark (D-Mo.), a member of Nye's committee, before a "Keep America Out of War" meeting at Carnegie Hall in New York City. Also on the program was Representative Maury Maverick (D-Tex.), another isolationist. Read the statements and consider the following questions: Was it really the sale of munitions that led America into World War I? Why might a 1935 audience have been especially receptive to charges that bankers were responsible for war? How successful were Nye, Clark, and others in enlisting the "overwhelming body of public sentiment" for neutrality legislation? If Roosevelt had strictly followed the spirit of the neutrality legislation, could American entry into World War II have been avoided?

SENATOR GERALD P. NYE (R-N. D.)

[The investigations of the Senate Munitions Committee have not been in vain;] truly worthwhile legislation will be forthcoming to meet the frightful challenge.

Out of this year of study has come tremendous conviction that our American welfare requires that great importance be given to the subject of our neutrality when others are at war.

Let us be frank before the next war comes as Wilson was frank after the last war was over.

Let us know that it is sales and shipments of munitions and contraband, and the lure of profits in them that will get us into another war.

If Morgan and the other bankers must get into another war, let them do it by enlisting in the Foreign Legion. That's always open.

SENATOR BENNETT CHAMP CLARK (D-MO.)

In these resolutions [calling for neutrality legislation] we propose that American citizens who want to profit from other people's war shall not be allowed again to entangle the United States.

We appeal to you to lend your efforts to the creation of an overwhelming body of public sentiment to bring about the firm establishment of that policy. The time for action is due and past due.

New York Times, 28 May, 1935. Copyright © 1935 by The New York Times Company. Reprinted by permission.

MAP EXERCISE

Fill in or identify the following on the blank maps provided. Use the text and the maps on pages 811, 814, and 833 as your sources.

1. Label the following: Japan, Manchuria, Pearl Harbor (Hawaii), Indochina.
2. Label the following: Soviet Union, Poland, Germany, Austria (incorporated into Germany), Czechoslovakia, Great Britain, Denmark, Norway, Netherlands, Belgium, France, Italy, and Spain.
3. Shade the areas that Germany and Italy controlled at the farthest extent of Axis control in Europe and North Africa.
4. Shade the areas that Japan controlled at its extent of farthest advance in World War II.

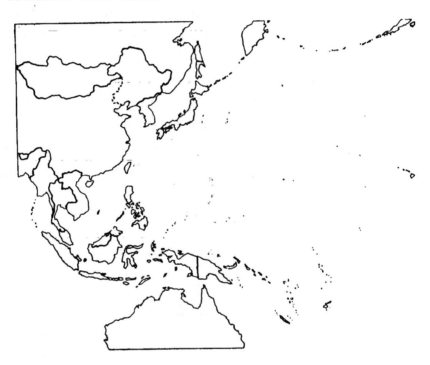

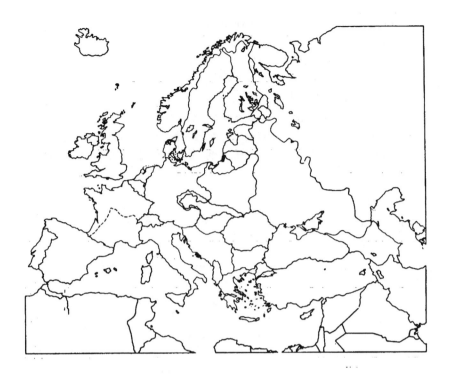

Interpretative Questions

Based on what you have filled in, answer the following. For some of the questions you will need to consult the narrative in your text for information or explanation.

1. How was Great Britain isolated during the height of Axis conquest?
2. Why was Germany initially concerned with avoiding a two-front war? Why did the United States aid the Soviet Union after the German invasion?
3. How did the Japanese expansion in Asia threaten U.S. interests?

SUMMARY

After World War I, the United States avoided international commitments but not international contact. Relations with Latin America improved; but in Asia and Europe, crises were brewing. The initial American reaction to the aggressive moves of Italy, Germany, and Japan was one of isolationism. Anxious to avoid involvement in another world war, the United States passed a series of Neutrality Acts; but as the Axis

295

aggressors became bolder, Roosevelt eased the nation closer and closer to war. The attack on Pearl Harbor blew away all isolationist remnants, and the nation entered World War II determined and unified.

CHAPTER SELF-TEST

After you have read the chapter in the text and done the exercises in the study guide, the following self-test can be taken to see if you understand the material you have covered. Answers appear at the end of the study guide.

Multiple Choice

Circle the letter of the response that best answers the question or completes the statement.

1. Throughout the 1920s, the makers of American foreign policy attempted to:
   a. win ratification of the Treaty of Versailles.
   b. promote U.S. membership in the League of Nations.
   c. retreat from international events and trade and renew the traditional policy of strict isolationism.
   d. expand America's role and interests in world affairs without assuming burdensome responsibilities.

2. At the Washington Conference of 1921, the United States sought negotiation of a treaty to:
   a. prevent a naval arms race in the Pacific Ocean.
   b. restructure the Open Door policy in China, allowing spheres of influence to separate nations.
   c. entice Japan to surrender colonial control over Korea.
   d. sanction Japanese dominance in East Asia.

3. The Kellog-Briand Pact of 1928, which "outlawed" war, suffered a fatal weakness in that it:
   a. contained a built-in expiration date.
   b. denied Germany the opportunity to join.
   c. lacked effective means of enforcement.
   d. involved only France and the United States.

4. According to the Dawes Plan of 1924, the United States would:
   a. scale down the amount of war debts owed by the former Allies to the United States.
   b. provide loans to Germany, enabling it to pay reparations to Britain and France.
   c. reduce tariff rates, allowing trading partners to increase exports and thus earn needed funds to repay debts.
   d. double its investments in Latin America, providing modern facilities to weaken the appeal of revolutionary groups in that region.

5. Official recognition of the Soviet regime in Russia by the American government in 1933 resulted in:
   a. an increased understanding and appreciation of the theories of communism by most Americans.
   b. plans by which the Soviet Union and the United States intended to contain expansion by fascist governments.
   c. significantly increased sales of American manufactured goods inside the Soviet Union.
   d. relatively little long-term change in the mutual mistrust that had characterized Soviet-American relations in the past.

6. According to the Neutrality Acts of 1935–1937,
   a. American citizens could travel only on American ships.
   b. no American arms could be sold to any belligerents.
   c. military goods could be sold on a cash-and-carry basis only.
   d. military goods could be sold to "victims" but not to "aggressors."

7. The "appeasement" of Hitler at the Munich Conference consisted of allowing German annexation of:
   a. Poland
   b. Belgium.
   c. the Netherlands.
   d. Czechoslovakia.

8. Which of the following was *not* done by President Roosevelt after the Nazi invasion (*blitzkrieg)* of western Europe?
   a. Imposing a "moral embargo" on arms sales to Russia
   b. Seeking additional defense expenditures from Congress
   c. Trading American destroyers for rights to build bases on British territory in the Western Hemisphere
   d. Inaugurating the first peacetime military draft in American history

9. In 1939, following the start of World War II in Europe, Congress:
   a declared war on Germany and Italy.
   b. allowed the United States to sell arms to belligerents on a "cash-and-carry" basis.
   c. directed the president to give weapons to the French and British and to transport them on U.S. ships.
   d. passed a Neutrality Act prohibiting the United States from having any economic contact with any belligerent nation.

10. The America First Committee was:
    a. an isolationist lobby that included such prominent Americans as Charles Lindbergh.
    b. a British organization working to convince the American public that the United States should enter the war to help England.
    c. a group within the German high command that tried to convince Hitler that he could not win unless he came to a truce with the Soviet Union and concentrated his efforts on the United States.
    d. an association of World War I veterans who lobbied Congress to significantly increase appropriations for the military so that America would be prepared for war.

11. The "lend-lease" program:
    a. placed "voluntary" U.S. troops under British command at British Empire outposts so that Great Britain could concentrate more troops in the European theater.
    b. allowed the United States to rent naval bases on Atlantic and Pacific islands from Great Britain "to provide for the mutual defense of the seas."
    c. funneled borrowed money indirectly to the "joint Atlantic war effort" through an elaborate arrangement involving banks in New York, Toronto, and London.
    d. provided a mechanism for President Roosevelt to get armaments to any nation "vital to the defense of the United States," mainly Great Britain, if the nation would promise to return the armaments after the crisis.

12. As of October 1941, U.S. naval vessels in the North Atlantic were:
    a. engaging in several spectacular surface battles with German battleships.
    b. escorting supply ships to England with orders to fire "on sight" at German submarines.
    c. prohibited from sailing into the "war zone," which extended 500 nautical miles from the coast of the British Isles.
    d. allowed to use long-range guns to provide "artillery support" for British commando operations in northern France.

13. In the August 1941 Atlantic Charter, President Roosevelt and Prime Minister Winston Churchill:
    a. decided that as soon as Nazi submarines were controlled in the Atlantic military forces should make the defeat of Japan in the Pacific the "highest priority."
    b. announced a set of de facto war aims with "common principles" that called for the "final destruction of the Nazi tyranny."
    c. formulated an offer to Hitler that they would not aid the Soviet Union if the Germans would agree to pull out of France and Belgium.
    d. agreed that the British would have principal responsibility for "command and control" in the European theater and that the United States would have it in Asia.

14. The militant Japanese prime minister and leader of the so-called war party was General:
    a. Hirohito.
    b. Yamamoto.
    c. Kamikaze.
    d. Tojo.

15. Militarily, the most significant U.S. loss in the attack on Pearl Harbor was the:
    a. sinking of eight battleships.
    b. sinking or disabling of four aircraft carriers.
    c. delay in obtaining a congressional declaration of war because of the demoralizing of the American public.
    d. delay in declaring war on Germany because of all the immediate anger focusing on Japan.

True/False

Read each statement carefully. Mark true statements "T" and false
statements "F."

___1.　Rather than being a pure isolationist, Senator Henry Cabot
　　　Lodge wanted the United States to exert its influence
　　　internationally but in a way that reflected U.S. interests and
　　　virtues and avoided obligations to other nations.

___2.　Secretary of State Charles Evans Hughes was the key figure in
　　　resisting efforts to significantly reduce the size of the American
　　　naval establishment after World War I.

___3.　The Dawes Plan of international finance granted France and
　　　Britain a moratorium on payment of war debts to the United
　　　States as long as Germany remained unable to make timely war
　　　reparations payments to them.

___4.　Herbert Hoover tried to improve U.S. relations with Latin
　　　America by declining to intervene militarily in the affairs of the
　　　neighboring nations.

___5.　When Japan invaded northern Manchuria and territories even
　　　deeper into China in 1931–1932, President Hoover cooperated
　　　with the League of Nations in imposing economic sanctions
　　　against Japanese aggression.

___6.　President Roosevelt's "Good Neighbor" policy renounced the
　　　approach of nonintervention that President Hoover had begun.

___7.　A major reason that the United States decided in 1933 to extend
　　　diplomatic recognition to the Soviet Union was that many
　　　Americans regarded Russia as a fertile source for trade
　　　expansion.

___8.　One point feeding isolationist sentiment in the 1930s was the
　　　Nye Committee charge that war profiteers in banking and
　　　industry had pressured the United States to enter World War I.

___9.　In the Spanish Civil War, Hitler and Mussolini supported
　　　Francisco Franco while the governments of France, Great
　　　Britain, and the United States provided military assistance to the
　　　republican cause.

___10.　The *Panay* incident brought the United States and Japan close to
　　　war in 1937 when an American battleship accidentally sank a
　　　Japanese patrol boat.

___11.　In the Munich accords of 1938, the French and British agreed to
　　　accept the German demands in Czechoslovakia in return for
　　　Hitler's promise to expand no further.

___12. The generally acknowledged "beginning of World War II" came with the German *blitzkrieg* against France and the low countries in June 1940.

___13. Agricultural Secretary Henry A. Wallace, President Roosevelt's choice for vice president in 1940, was unpopular with many Democrats because he was perceived as too liberal and too controversial.

___14. In the 1940 election, Republican nominee Wendell Willkie took a strong stance against President Roosevelt's policy of assisting France and Great Britain without actually entering the war.

___15. The U.S. Congress declared war on Germany and Italy *before* those nations could declare war on the United States.

Review Questions

These questions are to be answered with essays. This will allow you to explore relationships among individuals, events, and attitudes of the period under review.

1. How isolationist was the United States in the 1920s? Was the dual policy of economic penetration and arms limitation an effective approach?

2. Compare and contrast the American reactions to World Wars I and II. Explain the relationship between attitudes toward World War I and the isolationist sentiment and neutrality legislation of the 1930s.

3. How close to full involvement in World War II was the United States prior to the attack on Pearl Harbor? Was full entry likely?

CHAPTER TWENTY-EIGHT

America in a World at War

OBJECTIVES

A thorough study of Chapter 28 should enable you to understand:

1. The efforts of the federal government to mobilize the nation's economy for war production.
2. The impact of the war on American technology and science.
3. The effects of American participation in the war on the Depression and the New Deal.
4. The changes that wartime involvement brought for women and racial and ethnic minorities and for regional development.
5. The nature of work and leisure on the homefront.
6. The contribution of the U.S. military to victory in North Africa and Europe.
7. The contribution of the U.S. military to victory in the Pacific and Asia.

PERTINENT QUESTIONS

War on Two Fronts (pp. 809–815)

1. What was the basic Allied military strategy toward Japan?
2. What two American naval and air victories in mid-1942 stemmed the Japanese tide? What island victory early in 1943 ended Japanese chances at an offensive toward the south?
3. What did the North African and Italian offensives accomplish? How did the Soviet Union regard these efforts?
4. How did the United States react to the Holocaust? Why did the United States not do more to save the Jews?

The American Economy in Wartime (pp. 815–822)

5. How did World War II end the Great Depression and restore economic prosperity?
6. In what section of the nation was the economic impact especially dramatic? Why?

7. How did labor unions fare during the war?
8. What efforts did the national government make to regulate production, labor, and prices during the war?
9. How was World War II financed?
10. In what ways was World War II "a watershed for technological and scientific innovation"? How did American mass-production capability complement the technical advances? How did code breaking contribute to future computer technology?

Race and Gender in Wartime America (pp. 822–828)

11. Describe the demographic changes, economic gains, and military role of blacks in the war. What tensions resulted?
12. Describe the contributions American Indians made to the war effort. What impact did the war have on federal Indian policy?
13. How did the war effort affect Mexican Americans?
14. How were Japanese Americans treated during the war? What was done to atone for the treatment?
15. What impact did the war have on the legal and social status of Chinese Americans?
16. How were the women who filled war jobs treated? What obstacles did they face? What long-term consequences for the role of women in society and the work force were foreshadowed by the wartime experience?

Anxiety and Affluence in Wartime Culture (pp. 828–832)

17. How did the war spark a wave of consumerism reminiscent of the 1920s?
18. What was the most popular music of the war era? How did this new sound challenge racial taboos?
19. Compare and contrast military policy toward heterosexual and homosexual activity. Why was the treatment different?
20. What impact did the war have on the various programs of the New Deal?

The Defeat of the Axis (pp. 832–842)

21. Describe the Normandy invasion and the liberation of France. What role did air power play in preparing for the assault?
22. What role did Soviet forces play in the final defeat of Germany?
23. Describe the steady progression of American forces through the islands of the Pacific culminating at Okinawa. What did this experience seem to presage about the planned invasion of Japan?

24. Why did the United States decide to use the atomic bomb against Japan? Was it a wise decision? What have historians found?

IDENTIFICATION

Identify each of the following, and explain why it is important within the context of the chapter.
1. Douglas MacAuthur
2. Chester Nimitz
3. "Free French" forces
4. George C. Marshall
5. Dwight D. Eisenhower
6. George S. Patton
7. Benito Mussolini
8. "wildcat strikes"
9. Office of Price Administration (OPA)
10. Vannevar Bush
11. sonar and radar
12. V1 and V2
13. Enigma
14. A. Philip Randolph
15. Congress of Racial Equality (CORE)
16. *braceros*
17. "zoot-suit riots"
18. Issei and Nisei
19. "Rosie the Riveter"
20. WAAC and WAVE
21. "baby boom"
22. Benny Goodman/Glenn Miller
23. United Servicemen's Organization (USO)
24. Thomas E. Dewey
25. Harry S. Truman
26. Dresden raid
27. Battle of the Bulge
28. Burma Road
29. Chiang Kai-shek
30. Battle of Leyte Gulf
31. Iwo Jima
32. Okinawa
33. kamikaze
34. Albert Einstein

35. Manhattan Project

36. Hiroshima and Nagasaki

DOCUMENT

Read the text section entitled "African Americans and the War" (p. 822), paying careful attention to the discussion of the March on Washington movement, the establishment of the Fair Employment Practices Commission (FEPC), and the formation of the Congress of Racial Equality (CORE). The following excerpt is from a magazine article that A. Philip Randolph wrote after the FEPC was organized but before CORE was born. Consider the following questions: Could Randolph's remarks be interpreted as a threat that American blacks might not support the war effort unless they received assurances of better treatment? Was his description of the plight of blacks in the military and in defense plants accurate? Was Randolph right in saying that racial tension in America was worth "many divisions to Hitler and Hirohito"?

Though I have found no Negroes who want to see the United Nations[s][1] lose this war, I have found many who, before the war ends, want to see the stuffing knocked out of white supremacy and of empire over subject peoples. American Negroes, involved as we are in the general issues of the conflict, are confronted not with a choice but with the challenge both to win democracy for ourselves at home and to help win the war for democracy the world over.

There is no escape from the horns of this dilemma. There ought not to be escape. For if the war for democracy is not won abroad, the fight for democracy cannot be won at home. If this war cannot be won for the white peoples, it will not be won for the darker races.

Conversely, if freedom and equality are not vouchsafed the peoples of color, the war for democracy will not be won. Unless this double-barreled thesis is accepted and applied, the darker races will never whole-heartedly fight for the victory of the United Nations. That is why those familiar with the thinking of the American Negro have sensed his lack of enthusiasm, whether among the educated or uneducated, rich or poor, professional or nonprofessional, religious or secular, rural or urban, North, South, East, or West.

That is why questions are being raised by Negroes in church, labor union, and fraternal society; in poolroom, barbershop, schoolroom, hospital, hairdressing parlor, on college campus, railroad, and bus. One can hear such questions asked as these: What have Negroes to fight for? What's the difference between Hitler and that "cracker" Talmadge of Georgia?[2] Why has a man got to be Jim-Crowed to die for democracy? If you haven't got democracy yourself, how can you carry it to someone else?

What are the reasons for this state of mind? The answer is: discrimination, segregation, Jim Crow. Witness the Navy, the Army, the Air Corps; and also government services at Washington. In many parts of the South, Negroes in Uncle Sam's uniform are being put upon, mobbed, sometimes even shot down by civilian and military police, and, on occasion, lynched. Vested political interests in race prejudice are so deeply entrenched that to them winning the war against Hitler is secondary to preventing Negroes from winning democracy for themselves. This is worth many divisions to Hitler and Hirohito.[3] While labor, business, and farm are subjected to ceilings and floors and not allowed to carry on as usual, these interests trade in the dangerous business of race hate as usual.

When the defense program began and billions of the taxpayers' money were appropriated for guns, ships, tanks, and bombs, Negroes presented themselves for work only to be given the cold shoulder. North as well as South, and despite their qualifications, Negroes were denied skilled employment. Not until their wrath and indignation took the form of a proposed protest march on Washington, scheduled for July 1, 1941, did things begin to move in the form of defense jobs for Negroes. The march was postponed by the timely issuance (June 25, 1941) of the famous Executive Order No. 8802 by President Roosevelt. But this order and the President's Committee on Fair Employment Practice, established thereunder, have as yet only scratched the surface by way of eliminating discriminations on account of race or color in war industry. Both management and labor unions in too many places and in too many ways are still drawing the color line.

[1] The United Nations was the official name for the Allies. After the war, the name was used for the new international organization.
[2] Eugene Talmadge, racist governor of Georgia.
[3] Emperor of Japan.

Survey Graphic, November 1942.

MAP EXERCISE

Fill in or identify the following on the blank maps provided. Use the maps on pages 811, 814, and 833 of the text as your source.

1. Label the major belligerents, and indicate after each name whether the nation was Axis (AX) or Allied (AL). Circle the areas under Axis control.

2. Indicate with arrows the main American (AM) and British (GB) thrusts against the enemy in North Africa.

3. Label Normandy, Paris, and Berlin, and draw an arrow indicating the approximate line of advance of the Allied forces on the western front.

4. Label Stalingrad, and draw an arrow indicating the approximate line of advance of the Russian forces on the eastern front.

5. Label Japan, China, Manchuria, Burma, Indochina, Australia, Hawaii, the Philippines, Iwo Jima, and Okinawa.

6. Draw a light circle to indicate the approximate extent of the Japanese advance at its peak. Draw a darker circle around the area under Japanese control at the time the first atomic bomb was dropped.

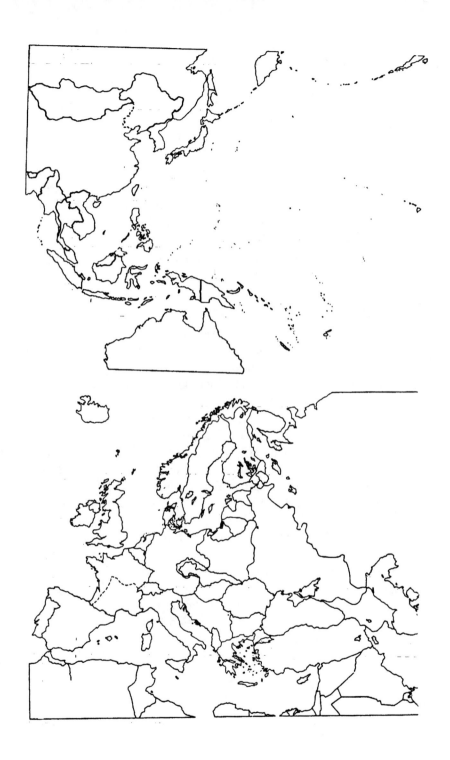

Interpretative Questions

Based on what you have filled in, answer the following. For some of the questions you will need to consult the narrative in your text for information or explanation.

1. How was Great Britain isolated during the height of Axis conquest?
2. Why was Allied control of North Africa considered so important?
3. Compare the Allied advance in World War II with that in World War I. (See the Map Exercise in Chapter 23.) Why did France and Russia suffer the most in both wars?
4. Why was the encircling of Japan the most effective strategy for the Allies in the Pacific?

SUMMARY

The United States entered World War II ideologically unified but militarily ill-prepared. A corporate-government partnership solved most of the production and manpower problems, and the massive wartime output brought an end to the Great Depression. Labor troubles, racial friction, and social tensions were not absent, but they were kept to a minimum. American productive capacity combined with scientific and technological developments to overwhelm the Axis. Roosevelt and the American generals made the decision that Germany must be defeated first, since it presented a more serious threat than Japan. Gradually American military might turned the tide in the Pacific and on the western front in Europe. The key to victory in Europe was an invasion of France that would coincide with a Russian offensive on the eastern front. Less than a year after D-Day, the war in Europe was over. In the Pacific, American forces—with some aid from the British and Australians—first stopped the Japanese advance and then went on the offensive. The strategy for victory moved Allied forces progressively closer to the Japanese homeland. Conventional bombing raids pulverized Japanese cities, and American forces were readied for an invasion that the atomic bomb made unnecessary.

CHAPTER SELF-TEST

After you have read the chapter in the text and done the exercises in the study guide, the following self-test can be taken to see if you understand the material you have covered. Answers appear at the end of the study guide.

Multiple Choice

Circle the letter of the response that best answers the question or completes the statement.

1. The Battle of Coral Sea:
    a. led to Japanese possession of Hong Kong.
    b. represented the first important victory of the Allies in the Pacific, stopping the Japanese southern offensive.
    c. enabled the United States to regain control of the central Pacific region.
    d. resulted in the Japanese takeover of the Dutch East Indies.

2. Rather than proceed with early plans for the invasion of France, American military leaders:
    a. agreed to Russian demands for establishment of a "second front" in Italy.
    b. agreed to British arguments to "soften" the edges of the Nazi empire with an offensive in northern Africa.
    c. concentrated almost exclusively on the war in the Pacific.
    d. decided an invasion of Europe should begin in Greece.

3. After the conclusion of the North African campaign, American and British forces turned their attention to the invasion of:
    a. southern France, toward Vichy.
    b. the Balkan region.
    c. Poland and eastern Europe.
    d. Italy, starting with Sicily.

4. Hitler's eastern offensive was shattered with his failure to capture the Russian stronghold of:
    a. Leningrad.
    b. Moscow.
    c. Kiev.
    d. Stalingrad.

5. The United States government responded to reports of the Holocaust, the Nazi campaign to exterminate European Jews, by:
   a. attempted bombings of concentration camp crematoria and railroad lines.
   b. limiting its attention at the time to the larger military goal of winning the war.
   c. admitting into the United States large numbers of Jewish refugees.
   d. transporting large numbers of Jewish refugees to Palestine.

6. The most profound immediate economic impact of World War II upon America was a(n):
   a. end to the decade-long problems of unemployment, depression, and industrial sluggishness.
   b. substantial reduction of the federal deficit with increased tax rates and revenues.
   c. tremendous increase in personal spending as workers used higher wages for newly available consumer goods.
   d. further imbalance in the nation's distribution of wealth.

7. African-American spokesman A. Philip Randolph threatened a massive march on Washington by blacks in the summer of 1941 to protest:
   a. the violent race riot in Detroit that had left twenty-five blacks dead.
   b. racial segregation in theaters and restaurants.
   c. racial segregation and limited assignments for blacks in the armed forces.
   d. discrimination against black workers in wartime industries.

8. For American women, wartime America provided thousands of new jobs in many fields, but mostly in:
   a. heavy industrial occupations vacated by men.
   b. clerical positions and other service jobs.
   c. domestic roles such as maid and seamstress.
   d. "camp follower" jobs such as waitress, taxi dancer, and prostitute.

9. In 1942 over 100,000 Japanese Americans were "interned" in government "relocation centers" because of:
   a. the revelation of Japanese sabotage at Pearl Harbor.
   b. their refusal to allow their young men to serve in U.S. military forces.
   c. fears of subversion compounded by ethnic prejudice.
   d. an order by the Supreme Court upon news of a plotted Japanese invasion of California.

10. The Allied movement toward Germany from the west met the last serious German resistance at the:
    a. raid on Dresden.
    b. Battle of the Bulge.
    c. Battle of Saint-Lô.
    d. capture of Cologne.

11. The invasion at Normandy, June 6, 1944:
    a. occurred approximately at the narrowest part of the English Channel.
    b. involved U.S. soldiers almost exclusively since most British troops were still pinned down in northern Italy.
    c. took about two months to dislodge German forces from the Normandy coast.
    d. was preceded by intensive bombardment of German fortifications and paratrooper drops behind the lines.

12. The Allied raid on Dresden, Germany:
    a. involved the use of incendiary bombs that killed over 100,000 people.
    b. was carried out by "Free French" commandos who liberated several thousand concentration camp survivors.
    c. was the first to demonstrate the effectiveness of unmanned guided missiles.
    d. diverted German attention so that Soviet forces could enter Berlin.

13. The leader of the nationalist Chinese forces allied with the United States in World War II was:
    a. Mao Zedong.
    b. Sun Yat-sen.
    c. Chou En-lai.
    d. Chiang Kai-shek.
    e. Lao Chungking.

14. The Battle of Leyte Gulf resulted in:
    a. the sinking of two American attack carriers and thus a significant delay in the invasion of the Philippines.
    b. a change in American strategy from reliance on battleships to more emphasis on lighter, faster ships such as destroyers and cruisers.
    c. severe damage to the British Pacific fleet from Hong Kong and thereby entrenched Japanese control of the Chinese mainland.
    d. a major American victory and a serious crippling of the Japanese navy in the largest naval engagement in history.

15. The "Manhattan Project" was the name given to the:
    a. intensive U.S. activities to develop an atomic bomb.
    b. consortium of Wall Street banks and investment firms that underwrote U.S. war bonds.
    c. top secret group that broke German and Japanese military codes and kept Allied commanders aware of Axis plans.
    d. effort to recruit experienced civilian corporate executives to work for the federal government's War Production Board.

True/False

Read each statement carefully. Mark true statements "T" and false statements "F."

___1.   Other than Pearl Harbor, the two greatest Japanese victories in World War II came in the Battles of Coral Sea and Midway.

___2.   The Soviet Union complained about the North African campaign because they believed that it had delayed a major second front in Europe by tying up American and British resources.

___3.   Because of the horror of the Holocaust, American and British command officers decided to make the liberation of Nazi concentration camps a higher priority than achieving the quickest possible end to the war.

___4.   The most profound impact of World War II on American economic life was finally to end the Great Depression, virtually wiping out unemployment.

___5.   Because of "no-strike" pledges and government arbitration rules, labor union membership declined during World War II.

___6.   In order not to slow down the economic recovery associated with the war effort, President Roosevelt and Congress decided to finance the war effort almost entirely by war bond drives without increasing income taxes.

___7.   During World War II, A. Philip Randolph was the administrator of the Office of Price Administration (OPA).

___8.   During World War II, the term *braceros* applied to Mexican workers who were allowed into the United States for a limited time to work at a specific job.

___9.   The nickname often applied to women who took wartime industrial jobs was "Homefront Hannah."

___10.   The domestic Japanese internment program during World War II moved virtually all Issei (first generation, unnaturalized) to camps but did not move Nisei (naturalized or native-born) unless they were the minor children of Issei.

___11. During World War II, President Roosevelt himself indicated that political emphasis should shift away from domestic reform, declaring that "Dr. New Deal" should give way to "Dr. Win-the-War."

___12. The Normandy invasion came in the spring of 1944, and Paris was liberated from Nazi control by the end of that summer.

___13. In January of 1945, the Soviet Union captured Poland and made peace with Nazi Germany, so the United States and Britain had to carry the bulk of the burden of finally conquering Berlin.

___14. The relatively easy conquest of Iwo Jima and Okinawa by naval and marine forces indicated that the Japanese military had nearly lost the means and will to resist.

___15. President Harry Truman's decision to drop atomic bombs on Japan was probably inevitable since as U.S. senator he had been chairman of the congressional committee that oversaw the atomic bomb development project.

Review Questions

These questions are to be answered with essays. This will allow you to explore relationships among individuals, events, and attitudes of the period under review.

1. Many of the broad strategy and social decisions of World War II are still debated. Describe the key issues involved in the second-front debate, the Japanese-American internment, and the dropping of atomic bombs. Were the right decisions made?

2. United States–Soviet relationships were tense throughout World War II despite the fact that the Soviets were on the Allied side. What issues caused those tensions? How important was the eastern front to the outcome of the war in Europe?

3. What was domestic life like in America during World War II? How were traditional racial, ethnic, and gender roles challenged?

CHAPTER TWENTY-NINE

The Cold War

OBJECTIVES

A thorough study of Chapter 29 should enable you to understand:
1. The background of United States relations with the Soviet Union before World War II.
2. The extent of collaboration between the United States and the Soviet Union during World War II, and the differences of view that developed between the two nations concerning the nature of the postwar world.
3. The meaning of the doctrine of containment, and the specific programs that implemented the concept.
4. The problems of postwar readjustment in the United States, especially controlling inflation.
5. The nature of the Fair Deal, its successes and failures.
6. The significance of China's becoming communist to American foreign policy in Asia.
7. The circumstances that led to United States participation in a "limited" war in Korea.
8. The reaction of American public opinion to President Harry Truman's handling of the "police action" in Korea, including his firing of General Douglas MacArthur.
9. The nature and extent of American fears of internal communist subversion during the early Cold War years.

PERTINENT QUESTIONS

Origins of the Cold War (pp. 844–848)

1. Describe the legacy of mistrust between the Soviet Union and the United States up to World War II. How did the view of the worl articulated by the United States contrast with the vision held by the Soviets and the British?
2. What were the accomplishments of the Casablanca and Tehran Conferences?

3. How did the Yalta Conference deal with the Polish and German questions? What differing views of the conference did the Soviets and Americans hold?

4. What was the basic United Nations plan that was agreed to by Roosevelt, Churchill, and Stalin at Yalta?

The Collapse of the Peace (pp. 849–858)

5. Compare and contrast Roosevelt's and Truman's attitudes toward Stalin and the Soviet Union. How did Potsdam reveal the difference?

6. How did the U.S. deal with China and Chiang Kai-shek in the postwar period? How did the situation in China shape U.S. policy toward Japan?

7. What led to the Truman Doctrine and containment? What pattern of foreign policy did the doctrine establish?

8. What motives led to the Marshall Plan? How successful was it?

9. How did the National Security Act of 1947 reorganize the administration of national security? What agencies were created?

10. Why did Stalin blockade Berlin? How did the United States respond, and what resulted?

11. What was the fundamental agreement central to the North Atlantic Treaty Organization (NATO)? How did the Soviet Union respond?

12. What events of 1949 thrust the Cold War into a new and seemingly more dangerous stage?

America After the War (pp. 858–863)

13. What factors combined to keep the United States from experiencing another depression after the war? What economic challenges did the nation face?

14. How did President Truman respond to the coal and railroad strikes in 1948?

15. How did reconversion affect the many women and minorities who had taken war-related jobs?

16. What was the Fair Deal? Why was it initially unsuccessful?

17. What strategy did Truman use to win the 1948 presidential election despite problems within the party?

18. What were the successes and failures of Truman's reform agenda after 1948?

The Korean War (pp. 863–867)

19. What caused the Korean War? How did it turn into a stalemate?
20. Why did Truman dismiss Douglas MacArthur? Why was the decision so controversial?
21. What social and economic effects did the Korean War have in America?

The Crusade Against Subversion (pp. 867–872)

22. Describe the factors and cases that combined to create the anticommunist paranoia that led to the rise of Joseph McCarthy.
23. How did Joseph McCarthy exploit the existing mood of hysteria? What sort of tactics did he use in his attacks on alleged subversion?
24. What personalities and policies led to the Republican victory in the presidential election of 1952?

IDENTIFICATION

Identify each of the following, and explain why it is important within the context of the chapter.

1. Dumbarton Oaks
2. "zone of occupation"
3. Chiang Kai-shek
4. Mao Zedong
5. George F. Kennan
6. hydrogen bomb
7. Atomic Energy Commission (AEC)
8. Federal Republic of Germany (West Germany)
9. Formosa (Taiwan)
10. NSC-68
11. GI Bill of Rights
12. Taft-Hartley Act
13. "right-to-work" laws
14. Dixiecrat Party
15. Thomas E. Dewey
16. Syngman Rhee
17. House Un-American Activities Committee
18. Hollywood blacklist
19. Alger Hiss
20. J. Edgar Hoover
21. Julius and Ethel Rosenberg

22. Adlai Stevenson
23. Dwight D. Eisenhower
24. Richard M. Nixon

DOCUMENT

Read the text section entitled "The Containment Doctrine" (p. 850) paying special attention to the discussion of the Truman Doctrine. The following is an excerpt from the March 12, 1947, speech in which Truman proclaimed the doctrine. He later remembered this program as "the turning point in America's foreign policy." Consider the following questions: What were the implications of a president unilaterally issuing what was, in essence, a treatylike commitment? Was the speech based on a false dichotomy between communist and "free" peoples? What in the speech foreshadows the economic containment approach of the Marshall Plan? Does American foreign policy continue to be based on the assumptions of containment and the Truman Doctrine?

I am fully aware of the broad implications involved if the United States extends assistance to Greece and Turkey, and I shall discuss these implications with you at this time.

One of the primary objectives of the foreign policy of the United States is the creation of conditions in which we and other nations will be able to work out a way of life free from coercion. This was a fundamental issue in the war with Germany and Japan. Our victory was won over countries which sought to impose their will, and their way of life, upon other nations.

The peoples of a number of countries of the world have recently had totalitarian regimes forced upon them against their will. The Government of the United States has made frequent protests against coercion and intimidation, in violation of the Yalta Agreement, in Poland, Rumania, and Bulgaria. . . .

At the present moment in world history nearly every nation must choose between alternative ways of life. The choice is too often not a free one.

One way of life is based upon the will of the majority, and is distinguished by free institutions, representative government, free elections, guarantees of individual liberty, freedom of speech and religion, and freedom from political oppression.

The second way of life is based upon the will of a minority forcibly imposed upon the majority. It relies upon terror and oppression, a controlled press and radio, fixed elections, and the suppression of personal freedoms.

I believe that it must be the policy of the United States to support free peoples who are resisting attempted subjugation by armed minorities or by outside pressures.

I believe that we must assist free peoples to work out their own destinies in their own way.

I believe that our help should be primarily through economic and financial aid, which is essential to economic stability and orderly political processes.

The world is not static and the status quo is not sacred. But we cannot allow changes in the status quo in violation of the Charter of the United Nations by such methods as coercion, or by such subterfuges as political infiltration. In helping free and independent nations to maintain their freedom, the United States will be giving effect to the principles of the Charter of the United Nations. . . .

Should we fail to aid Greece and Turkey in this fateful hour, the effect will be far reaching to the West as well as to the East. We must take immediate and resolute action. . . .

The seeds of totalitarian regimes are nurtured by misery and want. They spread and grow in the evil soil of poverty and strife. They reach their full growth when the hope of a people for a better life has died.

We must keep that hope alive.

The free peoples of the world look to us for support in maintaining their freedoms.

If we falter in our leadership, we may endanger the peace of the world—and we shall surely endanger the welfare of our own Nation.

Great responsibilities have been placed upon us by the swift movement of events.

I am confident that the Congress will face these responsibilities squarely.

MAP EXERCISE

Fill in or identify the following on the blank map provided. Use the map on page 854 of the text as your source.

1. Label all the countries.
2. Locate Berlin on the large map and show the approximate dividing line on the inset.
3. Label the Warsaw Pact nations.
4. Label the NATO nations.

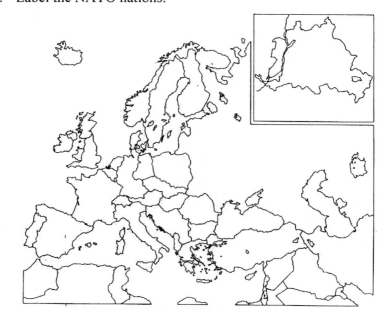

Interpretative Questions

Based on what you have filled in, answer the following. For some of the questions you will need to consult the narrative in your text for information or explanation.

1. Why was the form of government in Poland such a difficult issue to resolve? What sort of Polish state emerged?

2. Why was Germany divided? Why was Berlin divided even though it lay in the Russian zone? What was behind the decision of the United States, Great Britain, and France to merge their zones into a single nation?

3. Explain the policy of the Truman Doctrine. What was to be contained? Where? What developments were the catalyst for Truman's promulgation of the policy? What was the economic manifestation of the idea?

4. Why was the Soviet Union so suspicious of the West and so insistent on control of East Germany and the nations along the Soviet border? Were the Soviet concerns justified?

SUMMARY

The mutual hostility between the United States and the Soviet Union grew out of ideological incompatibility and concrete actions stretching back to World War I and before. The alliance of convenience and necessity against Germany temporarily muted the tensions, but disagreement over the timing of the second front and antagonistic visions of postwar Europe pushed the two nations into a "Cold War" only a few months after the victory over the Axis. The Cold War was marked by confrontation and the fear of potential military conflict. The United States vowed to contain communism by any means available.

Meanwhile, the American people, exhausted from a decade and a half of depression and war, turned away from economic reform. They were worried about the alleged Soviet threat in Europe, especially after the Soviet Union exploded its own atomic bomb in 1949. They were dismayed by the communist victory in China and perplexed by the limited war in Korea. Many Americans latched onto charges of domestic communist subversion as an explanation for the nation's inability to control world events. No one exploited this mood more effectively than Joseph McCarthy.

CHAPTER SELF-TEST

After you have read the chapter in the text and done the exercises in the study guide, the following self-test can be taken to see if you understand the material you have covered. Answers appear at the end of the study guide.

Multiple Choice

Circle the letter of the response that best answers the question or completes the statement.

1. According to the so-called postrevisionist view of some historians, as explained in "Debating the Past" (p. 856), the Cold War was principally the result of:
   a. aggressive Soviet policies of expansion in the postwar years.
   b. an American commitment to maintaining an "open door" for American trade in world markets.
   c. America's use of its nuclear monopoly to attempt to threaten and intimidate the Soviet Union.
   d. natural, predictable, and perhaps inevitable tensions and conflicts of interest between the world's two most powerful nations.

2. An issue on which basic disagreement remained for the Big Three at the Yalta Conference in February, 1945—one that led to only a vague compromise—was the:
   a. structure and elections for a postwar Polish government.
   b. need for Soviet participation in the war against Japan.
   c. return of some territory that the Soviet Union lost in the 1904 Russo-Japanese War.
   d. representation and powers of Security Council members of the United Nations.

3. According to the text, the Yalta accords represented a:
   a. fair and impartial settlement of the major postwar issues.
   b. general set of loose principles that sidestepped the most divisive issues.
   c. mutual acceptance of the idea of an "open" Europe.
   d. virtual "sellout" to Soviet demands for domination of Eastern Europe.

4. In contrast to Roosevelt, President Truman:
   a. insisted that the Russians could be persuaded to bargain.
   b. viewed Stalin as an essentially reasonable man.
   c. used a surface geniality to disguise his diplomatic intentions.
   d. believed in patient negotiations rather than confrontation.
   e. considered the Soviet Union fundamentally untrustworthy and viewed Stalin with suspicion.

5. Upon the eruption of a full-scale civil war in China between the forces of Chiang Kai-shek and Mao Zedong, the United States:
   a. sought a third, alternative faction to support.
   b. tried to reach an accommodation with Mao.
   c. continued to pump money and weapons to Chiang.
   d. refused to assist Chiang because his government was hopelessly incompetent and corrupt.

6. The Truman Doctrine committed the United States to a policy of:
   a. containing any attempt of communist expansion in areas of U.S. interest.
   b. appeasing the Soviet Union in order to avoid nuclear confrontation.
   c. initiating movements of national liberation in Greece and Turkey.
   d. overthrowing existing communist regimes.

7. The North Atlantic Treaty Organization (NATO) alliance:
   a. led to a quick reduction of America's military influence in Europe.
   b. spurred the Soviet Union to create the Warsaw Pact, an alliance with the communist governments in Eastern Europe.
   c. was not ratified by the United States Senate until after the Korean War.
   d. was composed of all the nations that had opposed Germany in World War II.

8. The Cold War took on a new tone in 1949 as a result of what *two* developments? (Choose two letters.)
   a. Soviet refusal to pull their occupation forces out of Iran
   b. Victory of communist forces in mainland China
   c. Communist overthrow of the pro-Western government in Greece
   d. Successful explosion of atomic weapons by the Soviet Union
   e. The reunification of North and South Korea

9. Representing a shift in foreign policy, the 1950 National Security Council report known as NSC-68 suggested:
    a. a massive airlift of supplies to break the communist blockade of West Berlin.
    b. United States assistance to Marshall Josip Broz Tito and the "unaligned" communist state of Yugoslavia.
    c. that the United States must take the initiative in resisting the expansion of communism in any location.
    d. creation of a defensive military alliance between the United States and the democratic nations of Western Europe.

10. The primary economic problem facing the United States in the immediate years following World War II was:
    a. serious inflation caused by heavy consumer demand and the lifting of wartime controls.
    b. return of recession with the cancellation of wartime contracts.
    c. unemployment caused by soldiers flooding the labor market.
    d. labor unrest and strikes protesting massive layoffs.

11. President Harry S. Truman's "Fair Deal" contained all of the following proposals *except:*
    a. expansion of Social Security benefits.
    b. significant tax reductions.
    c. federal aid to education.
    d. public housing and slum clearance projects.

12. The Labor-Management Relations Act of 1947, better known as the Taft-Hartley Act, outlawed the:
    a. closed shop, a workplace in which no one could be hired without first being a member of a union.
    b. union shop, a workplace in which workers must join a union after being hired.
    c. creation of open shops by passage of state "right-to-work" laws.
    d. stoppage of a strike by a presidential call for a "cooling-off" period.

13. The Taft-Hartley Act:
    a. was effectively killed by President Truman's veto.
    b. destroyed the political power of the labor movement.
    c. speeded the process of unionization in the South.
    d. represented a conservative backlash against New Deal reforms.

14. One of the factors contributing to Truman's stunning upset victory in the election of 1948 was:
    a. a serious splintering of the Republican Party into conservative and progressive factions.
    b. Truman's charge that the Republican-controlled Congress was "do-nothing, good-for-nothing."
    c. Truman's decision to conduct a quiet, reserved, statesmanlike campaign.
    d. Truman's shift from a liberal to a conservative stance on domestic issues.

15. The United States was able to win United Nations support for South Korea in the Korean War because the:
    a. war represented a clear case of aggression by North Korea.
    b. Security Council feared that the influence the new communist government in China would spread to Korea.
    c. Soviet Union was boycotting the Security Council at the time.
    d. United Nations had pledged itself to the creation of a unified, independent, and democratic Korea.

True/False

Read each statement carefully. Mark true statements "T" and false statements "F."

___1. At the Teheran Conference in November 1943, despite some tension and unresolved issues, Roosevelt and Stalin established a cordial personal relationship and the Soviet Union agreed to enter the war in the Pacific after the end of hostilities in Europe.

___2. At the Yalta Conference Stalin, Churchill, and Roosevelt agreed to the basic plan for the United Nations, which included a Security Council with permanent membership for the United States, Great Britain, France, China, and the Soviet Union.

___3. The communist victory in China in 1949 increased U.S. resolve to keep Japan economically weak so that the Japanese would not be tempted to renew aggression against China.

___4. The specific conflict that inspired President Truman to issue the "Truman Doctrine" involved a dispute between Poland and Hungary.

___5. The NSC-68 report was rejected by President Truman because it pointed out the high cost of containment and suggested that an arms race would delay economic recovery.

___6. Shortly after World War II there was a sharp rise in labor unrest marked by major strikes in the automobile, electrical, steel, and coal industries.

___7. As soon as Chiang Kai-shek and his forces fled to the island of Formosa (Taiwan), the United States officially recognized Mao Zedong's regime as the government of mainland China.

___8. The United States originally offered to include the Soviet Union and its Eastern European satellites in the Marshall Plan for economic recovery.

___9. Stalin blockaded access to Berlin so as to pressure the United States, Britain, and France to merge their zones of occupation into one unit as West Germany.

___10. President Truman's "Fair Deal," including the Taft-Hartley Act, was designed mainly as a conservative reaction to the reforms of the New Deal.

___11. After President Truman's unexpected victory in 1948, Congress quickly passed almost all of his "Fair Deal" agenda.

___12. Congress passed the "right-to-work" bill in order to guarantee work to any American unable to find a job, but it was killed by a Truman veto.

___13. The Korean War began in 1950 when military forces of the communist North invaded the pro-Western South.

___14. The investigations by the House Un-American Activities Committee (HUAC) exposed convincing evidence that communist agents had thoroughly infiltrated the U.S. Department of State during World War II while the United States was officially allied with the Soviet Union against Germany.

___15. Congress passed the McCarran Internal Security Act in order to prevent Senator Joseph McCarthy from extending his "Red Scare" hearing to the army.

Review Questions

These questions are to be answered with essays. This will allow you to explore relationships among individuals, events, and attitudes of the period under review.

1. The United States hotly protested Stalin's actions in Poland, East Germany, and the rest of Eastern Europe as a violation of the "one world" principle of the Atlantic Charter and a departure from the agreements reached at Yalta and Potsdam. Aside from pushing for creation of the United Nations, did American policy actually abide by its own principles, or was it just as much based on national self-interest as the Soviet Union's?

2. Explain how the Truman Doctrine, the Marshall Plan, NATO, support for Chiang Kai-shek, and the Korean War were based on the policy of containment. What did that policy concede to the Soviets? How did NSC-68 refine the doctrine? What geopolitical realities limited American options in Asia and Eastern Europe?

3. What general factors made the United States susceptible to the anticommunist paranoia of 1947 to 1953? What activities fanned the fury and paved the way for the rise of Joseph McCarthy?

CHAPTER THIRTY
The Affluent Society

OBJECTIVES

A thorough study of Chapter 30 should enable you to understand:

1. The strengths and weaknesses of the economy in the 1950s and early 1960s.
2. How new technologies and expanded mass communication were changing America.
3. The problems faced by the "other America."
4. The changes in the American lifestyle and culture in the 1950s.
5. The impact of the Supreme Court's desegregation decision and the early civil rights movement.
6. The characteristics of Dwight D. Eisenhower's middle-of-the-road domestic policy.
7. The new elements of American foreign policy introduced by Secretary of State John Foster Dulles.
8. The rationale for the initial United States involvement in Vietnam.
9. The interests of the U.S. in the Middle East and the crises of the region.
10. The sources of United States difficulties in Latin America.
11. The reasons for new tensions with the Soviet Union toward the end of the Eisenhower administration.

PERTINENT QUESTIONS

The Economic "Miracle" (pp. 875–879)

1. What caused the low unemployment rate and the great growth in GNP from 1945 to 1960? How widespread was the prosperity?
2. What factors combined to stimulate the rapid population expansion and economic growth that characterized the American West in the post–World War II era?

3. What major advances in benefits did the major labor unions obtain in the late 1940s and 1950? What challenges did the labor movement face?

The Explosion of Science and Technology (pp. 879–886)

4. Describe how the prewar groundwork in antibiotics and immunization flowered after 1945. What major diseases were virtually eliminated in the U.S.?
5. How had the use of computers expanded by the early 1950s? What company dominated the computer market in these years?
6. Describe the process by which the U.S. developed reliable ICBMs. Why was this military effort so critical to the space program?
7. What impact did the Soviet launching of *Sputnik* have in the U.S.?
8. After the U.S. won the race to the moon, what direction did the American space program take?

People of Plenty (pp. 887–896)

9. Explain the expanded role of advertising and consumer credit. Why can it be said that the prosperity of the 1950s and 1960s was substantially consumer-driven?
10. What was the appeal of Levittown and similar suburban developments? How did typical suburbs transform family life and shape women's attitudes?
11. Describe how commercial television drew on the concepts and corporate structure of the radio era. How did the emergence of TV as the dominant medium reshape radio?
12. Why can it be said that television "was central to the culture of the postwar era"? How did the medium simultaneously unify and alienate Americans?
13. In what ways did several writers of the 1950s reflect the growing tensions between an organized, bureaucratic society and the tradition of individualism?
14. How did black music influence the development of rock 'n' roll? To what extent was the audience multiracial?

The Other America (pp. 897–899)

15. What was the extent of "hard core" poverty in the otherwise prosperous nation? What groups predominated in this "hard core"?
16. Why was so much of rural America still mired in poverty as late as 1960?

17. Describe the process that led to large pockets of poverty-stricken minorities in northern and southwestern cities. Why did so many of these people remain poor at a time of growing national affluence?

The Rise of the Civil Rights Movement (pp. 899–904)

18. How did the political power structure of the Deep South respond to the *Brown* v. *Board of Education* (and *Brown II*) ruling? What was the result?
19. What was the importance of the Montgomery, Alabama, bus boycott?
20. What philosophy shaped Martin Luther King, Jr.'s approach to civil rights protest? How did he become the principal leader and symbol of the movement?
21. What were the key factors that converged in the postwar period to ignite the civil rights movement?

Eisenhower Republicanism (pp. 904–906)

22. From what segment of society did President Dwight Eisenhower draw most of the members of his administration? How did these men and women differ from their 1920s counterparts of similar background?
23. Contrast Eisenhower's attitude toward new social legislation with his approach to existing programs.
24. What led to the demise of Senator Joseph McCarthy and the end of the Red Scare?

Eisenhower, Dulles, and the Cold War (pp. 906–911)

25. Why did John Foster Dulles move the United States toward the policy of massive retaliation?
26. How did the Korean War end?
27. Describe Ho Chi Minh's background, motives, and sources of support in his defeat of the French. Why did the Truman administration support the French?
28. Why did Ngo Dinh Diem and his government in the southern part of Vietnam refuse to participate in the reunification elections called for by the Geneva accords of 1954?
29. Why was the United States so committed to friendliness and stability in the Middle East? How was this approach implemented in Iran?
30. What led to the Suez Crisis of 1956? What position did the United States take?

31. What led to increasing animosity toward the United States on the part of many Latin Americans? What did the Guatemalan incident reveal about American intentions?
32. What led to Fidel Castro's rise in Cuba? How did the United States deal with his new regime?
33. What did the Hungarian Revolution and the U-2 incident reveal about the nature of the United States–Soviet relationship in the late 1950s and into 1960?

IDENTIFICATION

Identify each of the following, and explain why it is important within the context of the chapter.

1. "baby boom"
2. Los Angeles
3. AFL-CIO
4. penicillin
5. Jonas Salk/Albert Sabin
6. DDT
7. transistors/integrated circuits
8. UNIVAC
9. H-bomb
10. *Explorer I*
11. NASA
12. "astronaut"
13. Apollo program
14. space shuttle
15. Walt Disney
16. Benjamin Spock
17. "soap operas"
18. *Father Knows Best*
19. "beats/beatniks"
20. Elvis Presley
21. Motown Records
22. "disk jockey"
23. "juke box"
24. Michael Harrington
25. "juvenile delinquency"
26. "massive resistance"
27. Earl Warren
28. White Citizens' Councils

29. Little Rock Central High School
30. Rosa Parks
31. Southern Christian Leadership Conference (SCLC)
32. Federal Interstate Highway Act of 1956
33. Ngo Dinh Diem
34. Nikita Khrushchev
35. "military-industrial complex"

DOCUMENT

Read the text section entitled "France, America, and Vietnam" (p. 907), paying close attention to the discussion of how the United States got involved in Southeast Asia. The following document is from the so-called *Pentagon Papers,* a classified Defense Department study of the Vietnam conflict up to 1967. The study was leaked to the press in 1971 amid considerable controversy, including a landmark Supreme Court decision on freedom of the press. The massive report details American involvement in Indochina stretching back into World War II. The study clearly indicates that the government consistently misled Congress and the American people about the extent of American involvement and the gravity of the situation. This document is an excerpt from an official National Security Council (NSC) statement of policy approved by President Truman on June 25, 1952—two years before the fall of Dien Bien Phu. Read the document, and consider these questions: How might the Korean experience have shaped NSC thinking? Was the United States really defending the "free world" in Vietnam, or was it protecting its own interests and pursuing an obsession with fighting communism whatever its source? Was the Geneva agreement really doomed from the beginning?

OBJECTIVE

1. To prevent the countries of Southeast Asia from passing into the communist orbit, and to assist them to develop the will and ability to resist communism from within and without and to contribute to the strengthening of the free world.

GENERAL CONSIDERATIONS

2. Communist domination, by whatever means, of all Southeast Asia would seriously endanger in the short term, and critically endanger in the longer term, United States security interests.

   a. The loss of any of the countries of Southeast Asia to communist control as a consequence of overt or covert Chinese Communist aggression would have critical psychological, political and economic consequences. In the absence of effective and timely counteraction, the loss of any single country would probably lead to relatively swift submission to or an alignment with

330

communism by the remaining countries of this group. Furthermore, an alignment with communism of the rest of Southeast Asia and India, and in the longer term, of the Middle East (with the probable exceptions of at least Pakistan and Turkey) would in all probability progressively follow. Such widespread alignment would endanger the stability and security of Europe.

b. Communist control of all of Southeast Asia would render the U.S. position in the Pacific offshore island chain precarious and would seriously jeopardize fundamental U.S. security interests in the Far East.

c. Southeast Asia, especially Malaya and Indonesia, is the principal world source of natural rubber and tin, and a producer of petroleum and other strategically important commodities. The rice exports of Burma and Thailand are critically important to Malaya, Ceylon and Hong Kong and are of considerable significance to Japan and India, all important areas of free Asia.

d. The loss of Southeast Asia, especially of Malaya and Indonesia, could result in such economic and political pressures in Japan as to make it extremely difficult to prevent Japan's eventual accommodation to communism. . . .

3. The danger of an overt military attack against Southeast Asia is inherent in the existence of a hostile and aggressive Communist China, but such an attack is less profitable than continued communist efforts to achieve domination through subversion. The primary threat to Southeast Asia accordingly arises from the possibility that the situation in Indochina may deteriorate as a result of the weakening of the resolve of, or as a result of the inability of the governments of France and of the Associated States to continue to oppose the Viet Minh rebellion, the military strength of which is being steadily increased by virtue of aid furnished by the Chinese Communist regime and its allies.

MAP EXERCISE

Fill in or identify the following on the blank map provided. Use the map on page 928 and the narrative in your text as your source.

1. Identify and label the following countries: Cuba and Guatemala.
2. Identify and label the following U.S. interests: Florida, Panama Canal zone, Puerto Rico.

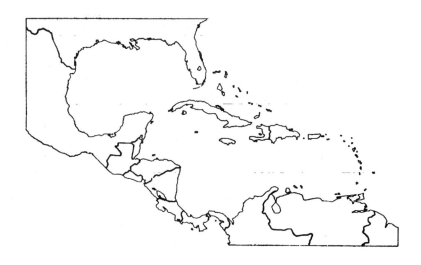

Interpretative Questions

Based on what you have filled in, answer the following. For some of the
questions you will need to consult the narrative in your text for
information or explanation.

1. Why was the United States so concerned about the ideology of
   those in control of Guatemala in 1954? What action did the
   United States take?
2. What was the pre-1959 U.S. relationship with Cuba? How did
   the U.S. reaction to Fidel Castro evolve?

SUMMARY

From the late 1940s through the 1950s, the United States experienced
continued economic growth and low unemployment. Most of the nation
participated in the prosperity and agreed about the beneficence of
American capitalism and consumerism. New technologies in medicine
and computing improved lives and began to reshape business.
Television presented a unified and sanitized American culture to
millions, and radio brought rock 'n' roll to the masses. Only a few
intellectuals questioned the rampant consumerism and the values of the
growing corporate bureaucracies. Those who lived in the "other
America" of rural and core-city poverty were generally ignored by the
affluent and the intellectuals. The politics of the period, symbolized by
President Eisenhower, the cautious war hero, reflected the popular
contentment. Blacks, inspired by the *Brown* school desegregation

decision, began the protests that would bring the civil rights revolution of the 1960s. Locked into a policy of containment and a rigidly dualistic world view, the United States was less successful in its overseas undertakings. Despite a string of alliances, an awesome nuclear arsenal, and vigorous use of covert operations, the nation often found itself unable to shape world events to conform to American desires.

CHAPTER SELF-TEST

After you have read the chapter in the text and done the exercises in the study guide, the following self-test can be taken to see if you understand the material you have covered. Answers appear at the end of the study guide.

Multiple Choice

Circle the letter of the response that best answers the question or completes the statement.

1. America's economic prosperity in the 1950s was fueled by:
   a. increased public funding of schools, housing, veteran's benefits, welfare, and interstate highways.
   b. the continuation of military spending at almost wartime levels.
   c. the "baby boom" and rapid expansion of the suburbs.
   d. All of the above
   e. None of the above
2. All of the following contributed to the rise of the modern West *except:*
   a. state government investment in Universities.
   b. federal spending on dams, highways, and other infrastructure projects.
   c. the conversion of most of the region's military plants to civilian production.
   d. the increasing number of automobiles and the rising demand for petroleum.
   e. warm, dry climate.
   f. No exceptions; all of these factors contributed.
3. The vaccines developed by Jonas Salk and Albert Sabin virtually eliminated what disease in America?
   a. Smallpox
   b. Polio
   c. Tuberculosis
   d. Influenza

4. The company that became the world leader in computers by the late 1950s and 1960s was:
   a. General Electric (GE).
   b. Remington Rand (RR).
   c. American Telephone and Telegraph (AT&T).
   d. International Business Machines (IBM).
   e. None of the above

5. Life in suburbia was especially attractive to many American families in the 1950s because, in contrast to the central cities, the suburbs provided:
   a. variety and excitement in lifestyles and entertainment.
   b. harmonious racial integration in neighborhoods and schools.
   c. greater opportunities for attending cultural facilities such as symphonies and museums.
   d. larger, safer, and more private homes.

6. Which region of the United States experienced the most dramatic change as a result of economic growth in the period from World War II to about 1960?
   a. the South
   b. the North
   c. the East
   d. the West
   e. the Midwest

7. According to Dr. Benjamin Spock, the highly regarded child care expert of the late 1940s and 1950s, women could become better mothers by:
   a. fulfilling their career and professional goals.
   b. staying home and focusing on the needs of their children.
   c. sharing the role of parenting more equally with the fathers.
   d. working to supplement income and increase family purchasing power.

8. During the 1950s, the television industry:
   a. actually affected only a very small percentage of the total population.
   b. served to encourage individuality and an independence in values and beliefs among members of the white middle class.
   c. served primarily as a culturally unifying force since millions of Americans viewed standard fare.
   d. failed to attract enough interest from commercial advertisers to be financially successful.

9. The United States accomplished which of the following feats *before* the Soviet Union? (Choose one or more letters as appropriate.)
   a. Launching a satellite into outer space
   b. Initiating a manned orbit of the earth
   c. Landing men on the surface of the moon
   d. None of the above

10. Which of the following was a situation comedy that portrayed the white, suburban, middle-class image typical of the TV of the 1950s?
    a. *The Organization Man*
    b. *The Honeymooners*
    c. *Amos 'n Andy*
    d. *Father Knows Best*

11. The principal message of the "beats" (or beatniks), young poets and writers of the 1950s:
    a. criticized the sterility and conformity of American life and culture.
    b. warned of the dangers of international communism.
    c. offered a romantic and nostalgic vision of the past.
    d. urged rededication by politicians to the American dream.

12. Michael Harrington's *The Other America* (1962) captured the nation's attention by focusing on:
    a. technological advances.
    b. the continuing problem of poverty.
    c. future political prospects.
    d. the network of organized crime.
    e. working women.

13. The *Brown v. Board of Education* decision of 1954:
    a. was strongly endorsed by President Eisenhower.
    b. bitterly divided the justices of the Supreme Court.
    c. provided a specific timetable and guidelines for school integration.
    d. encountered strong opposition and delay tactics throughout the South.

14. The arrest of Rosa Parks in Montgomery, Alabama, led to a boycott by blacks of the city's:
    a. lunch counters.
    b. department stores.
    c. bus lines.
    d. public schools.
    e. court system.

15. In domestic affairs, President Dwight D. Eisenhower:
    a. worked to expand government's involvement in and control of the economy.
    b. exercised strong personal leadership to pass his social agenda through Congress.
    c. expanded public development of natural resources through TVA-type projects.
    d. permitted the survival, and sometimes the expansion, of the social programs that were already in place when he took office.

True/False

Read each statement carefully. Mark true statements "T" and false statements "F."

___1.   From 1945 to 1960 the American economy grew significantly because of rapid population growth, but the growth was misleading because the economy was actually declining in real per capita dollars.

___2.   In 1955 the American Federation of Labor (AFL) and the Congress of Industrial Organizations (CIO) split due to philosophical differences and did not reunify until the early 1980s.

___3.   In the 1950s, the Levittown development near New York City symbolized the rapid postwar growth of suburban, single-family-house neighborhoods.

___4.   By the late 1950s televisions had become, according to one report, more common than refrigerators in American homes.

___5.   The Russian launching of the space satellite *Sputnik* before the U.S. had launched its own satellite alarmed Americans and led not only to an increased focus on the nation's space program but also to increased emphasis on science education in the schools.

___6.   Although the *Brown* v. *Board of Education of Topeka* decision on school integration was not popular with most white southerners, most states and school districts bowed to pressure from the Eisenhower administration and implemented the ruling within about three years.

___7.   The incident that thrust Martin Luther King, Jr., into prominence as a leader of the civil rights movement was the black boycott of the segregated bus system in Montgomery, Alabama.

___8.   The president of General Motors Company who declared that "what was good for our country was good for General Motors, and vice versa," became secretary of defense for President Eisenhower.

___9.   Although President Eisenhower was a Republican who remained personally popular, the Democratic Party held control of both houses of Congress from 1954 to the end of the Eisenhower administration and well beyond that time.

___10.   The political demise of Senator Joseph McCarthy was closely associated with his attacks on the army.

___11.   Secretary of State John Foster Dulles believed that the U.S. military had placed too much reliance on the atomic bomb and "massive retaliation" strategy; he therefore began to shift military spending priorities toward "flexible response."

___12.   The Eisenhower administration maintained good relations with Castro's Cuba, and tensions did not develop until John Kennedy enlisted the CIA to try to overthrow Castro.

___13.   The Korean War ended very early in the Eisenhower administration with an armistice that left the Korean peninsula divided at the 38th parallel.

___14.   For approximately nine years after the end of World War II, the United States provided military aid to the French government in Vietnam in its struggle against the anticolonial nationalist forces led by communist Ho Chi Minh.

___15.   In 1948 when the Jews in Palestine proclaimed the existence of the independent nation of Israel, President Truman delayed for several months extending diplomatic recognition to the new nation because he did not want to offend the oil-rich Arab nations.

Review Questions

These questions are to be answered with essays. This will allow you to explore relationships among individuals, events, and attitudes of the period under review.

1.   Analyze the causes and consequences of the economic boom of the 1950s. Explain who was left out and why.

2.   Did the assumptions of containment lead the United States into unwise commitments and actions in Southeast Asia, Latin America, and the Middle East, or was the nation acting prudently in response to hostile communist expansionism?

3. What new cultural developments accompanied the prosperity and suburbanization of the 1950s? How did intellectuals regard the highly organized and homogenized new society?
4. With focus on youth culture and race relations, compare and contrast the jazz and swing movements of the 1920s to 1940s with the rock 'n' roll phenomenon of the mid-1950s to mid-1960s.

CHAPTER THIRTY-ONE
The Ordeal of Liberalism

OBJECTIVES

A thorough study of Chapter 31 should enable you to understand:

1. The new directions of domestic reform manifested by John Kennedy's New Frontier program.
2. The new elements added to Kennedy's program by Lyndon Johnson's Great Society proposals.
3. The reasons why the African-American civil rights movement became increasingly assertive in the 1960s.
4. The significance of Martin Luther King, Jr., and Malcolm X to the civil rights movement.
5. The new elements that Kennedy introduced in both the nation's defense strategy and its foreign policy.
6. The background and sequence of events leading to the Cuban missile crisis.
7. The reasons for U.S. involvement in the Vietnam War and why it was unsuccessful.
8. The growing domestic opposition to the war in Vietnam and reasons why the 1968 Tet offensive had such a critical impact on American domestic politics.

CHRONOLOGY OF THE WAR IN INDOCHINA

Because American involvement in Indochina stretched from the 1940s through the 1970s, the material is in several chapters. This chronology will help you see the entire span of the Vietnam War.

1945–1954	Ho Chi Minh leads fight against French colonialism
1950	United States finances most of the French effort
1954	French defeated at Dien Bien Phu
	Geneva Conference partitions Indochina
1956	President Diem refuses to hold reunification elections
1960	National Liberation Front (NLF) (Viet Cong) organized

1963	Diem deposed and killed
	About 15,000 American advisers in South Vietnam
1964	Gulf of Tonkin Resolution
1965	American bombing of North Vietnam begins
	180,000 American troops in Vietnam by year's end
1966	Fulbright hearings begin
	300,000 American troops in Vietnam
1967	Major antiwar protests under way
	500,000 American troops in Vietnam
1968	
January	Tet offensive
March	Johnson announces bombing pause and his withdrawal from presidential race
1969	American troop strength peaks at 540,000
1970	
May	Cambodia invaded
	Kent State and Jackson State incidents
December	Gulf of Tonkin Resolution repealed
1971	Pentagon Papers released
1972	
Spring	Hanoi and Haiphong bombed
Fall	American troop strength down to 60,000
December	"Christmas bombings"
1973	Cease-fire; Paris accords
1975	Last American officials leave from U.S. embassy in Saigon
	Vietnam unified by victory of northern forces
1978	Vietnam invades Cambodia
	China invades Vietnam

PERTINENT QUESTIONS

Expanding the Liberal State (pp. 914–921)

1. Describe John F. Kennedy's background and his plans for domestic legislation. How did his New Frontier fare?
2. Describe the events surrounding the Kennedy assassination. What are the varying opinions about who was responsible?

3. How did Lyndon Johnson differ from Kennedy in personality and in the ability to influence Congress?

4. What were the purposes of Medicare and Medicaid? Why were they controversial?

5. What agency was the "centerpiece" of the Great Society? What new approach tried to involve the poor themselves in shaping the programs?

6. Who opposed federal aid to education? How did Johnson's legislation manage to circumvent much of the opposition?

7. How did the effort to fund both the Great Society and a great military establishment affect the federal budget?

8. What did the Great Society accomplish?

The Battle for Racial Equality (pp. 921–927)

9. Describe the increasing civil rights activism of the early 1960s. How did this protest movement affect public policy?

10. What events prompted passage of the Civil Rights Act of 1965 (Voting Rights Act)?

11. How did the focus of racial issues and the locus of the civil rights movement change in the mid- to late 1960s?

12. Describe the race riots of 1964 to 1967. What response did the Commission on Civil Disorder suggest? How did many white Americans react to the disorder?

13. What did "black power" mean? What impact did it have on the civil rights movement and on the attitudes of American blacks in general?

"Flexible Response" and the Cold War (pp. 927–930)

14. How did John F. Kennedy's approach to foreign policy contrast with Eisenhower's? What specific programs illustrated that difference?

15. What were the purpose and the result of the Bay of Pigs invasion?

16. What precipitated the Cuban missile crisis? How was it resolved? What was its legacy?

17. Why did Lyndon Johnson send troops to the Dominican Republic? Was the action reminiscent of the interventions in the days of the Roosevelt Corollary?

Vietnam (pp. 930–938)

18. Describe the Diem regime and its war effort up to 1963. What led to the coup and assassination that ended his rule?

19. Recount the stages of Johnson's escalation of the Vietnam War up to 1967. Why did the conflict become a "quagmire"?
20. Why did America's twofold strategy of "attrition" and "pacification" fail?
21. Where did domestic opposition to the war originate? How did it spread?
22. How did involvement in Vietnam affect the American economy?

The Traumas of 1968 (pp. 938–942)

23. What effect did the Tet offensive have on American public opinion concerning the war and on the course of the 1968 presidential election?
24. How did the nation respond to the assassination of Martin Luther King, Jr.?
25. What anxieties did Richard Nixon and George Wallace exploit in the 1968 presidential election?
26. How have historians differed in their explanations for the continuing involvement of the United States in Vietnam despite bleak prospects for victory?

IDENTIFICATION

Identify each of the following, and explain why it is important within the context of the chapter.

1. Lee Harvey Oswald
2. Warren Commission
3. Barry Goldwater
4. Robert Weaver
5. Immigration Act of 1965
6. sit-in
7. Student Nonviolent Coordinating Committee (SNCC)
8. Congress of Racial Equality (CORE)
9. "I have a dream"
10. "Freedom Summer"
11. "affirmative action"
12. Black Panthers
13. Malcolm X
14. Green Berets
15. Alliance for Progress
16. Berlin Wall
17. Vietminh
18. Viet Cong/National Liberation Front

19. Gulf of Tonkin Resolution
20. J. William Fulbright
21. Robert F. Kennedy
22. Hubert Humphrey

DOCUMENT

Read the text section entitled "Urban Violence" (p. 925). The document below is drawn from the 1967 report of the National Commission on Civil Disorders, often called the Kerner Commission because it was headed by Governor Otto Kerner of Illinois. Consider the following questions: Why did the riots come at a time when blacks were making legal gains? How would conservative whites react to the commission's findings? What traditional American values does the report affront? What values does it affirm? More than thirty years later, how close is America to realizing the vision of the Kerner Commission? Does the elimination of racism remain "the major unfinished business of this nation"?

This is our basic conclusion: Our nation is moving toward two societies, one black, one white—separate and unequal.

Reaction to last summer's disorders has quickened the movement and deepened the division. Discrimination and segregation have long permeated much of American life; they now threaten the future of every American.

This deepening racial division is not inevitable. The movement apart can be reversed. Choice is still possible. Our principal task is to define that choice and to press for a national resolution.

To pursue our present course will involve the continuing polarization of the American community and, ultimately, the destruction of basic democratic values.

The alternative is not blind repression or capitulation to lawlessness. It is the realization of common opportunities for all within a single society.

This alternative will require a commitment to national action—compassionate, massive and sustained, backed by the resources of the most powerful and the richest nation on this earth. From every American it will require new attitudes, new understanding, and, above all, new will.

The vital needs of the nation must be met; hard choices must be made, and, if necessary, new taxes enacted.

Violence cannot build a better society. Disruption and disorder nourish repression, not justice. They strike at the freedom of every citizen. The community cannot—it will not—tolerate coercion and mob rule.

Violence and destruction must be ended—in the streets of the ghetto and in the lives of people.

Segregation and poverty have created in the racial ghetto a destructive environment totally unknown to most white Americans.

What white Americans have never fully understood—but what the Negro can never forget—is that white society is deeply implicated in the ghetto. White institutions created it, white institutions maintain it, and white society condones it.

It is time now to turn with all the purpose at our command to the major unfinished business of this nation. It is time to adopt strategies for action that will produce quick and visible progress. It is time to make good the promises of American democracy to all citizens—urban and rural, white and black, Spanish-surname, American Indian, and every minority group.

National Commission on Civil Disorders, 1967.

MAP EXERCISE

Fill in or identify the following on the blank map provided. Use the map on page 931 of the text as your source.

1. All countries.
2. Mekong Delta and Gulf of Tonkin.
3. Hanoi, Saigon, Haiphong, Phnom Penh, and Bangkok.
4. DMZ.

Interpretative Questions

Based on what you have filled in, answer the following. For some of the
questions you will need to consult the narrative in your text for
information or explanation.

1. How did the United States get dragged into the conflict in
   Southeast Asia? How did Vietnam get divided?
2. From what internal and external sources did the Viet Cong
   receive their support? How did this make them so difficult to
   defeat?
3. What trap of competing factors kept Lyndon Johnson from either
   withdrawing or further escalating the war? How did the
   geographic position of Indochina in relation to China affect this
   trap?

SUMMARY

The 1960s began with John F. Kennedy squeezing out one of the narrowest presidential victories in United States history. Three years later, he was dead, and it was up to Lyndon Johnson to carry through his liberal legacy. The first three years of Johnson's presidency were legislatively one of the most productive periods ever, as Congress passed many of the civil rights, health, education, and welfare measures of the Great Society. In 1961, the nation bungled an attempt to dislodge Castro from Cuba, and a year and half later, the world came to the brink of nuclear war during the Cuban missile crisis. By the latter half of the decade, the foreign policy focus had moved halfway around the world. By the end of 1967, the United States had been involved in Vietnam for over twenty years and had 500,000 troops in the Southeast Asia war zone. The war in Vietnam had become the central issue of American politics.

CHAPTER SELF-TEST

After you have read the chapter in the text and done the exercises in the study guide, the following self-test can be taken to see if you understand the material you have covered. Answers appear at the end of the study guide.

Multiple Choice

Circle the letter of the response that best answers the question or completes the statement.

1. John F. Kennedy made an attractive presidential candidate in 1960 for all of the following reasons *except* his:
   a. family wealth and prestige.
   b. past accomplishments as a war hero and a prize-winning author.
   c. personal eloquence, wit, and charisma.
   d. promise to keep the nation on the course of the 1950s.

2. In contrast to Kennedy, President Lyndon B. Johnson:
   a. rejected the concept of dynamic governmental activism.
   b. possessed a shy and reticent personality.
   c. displayed remarkable skill in influencing Congress.
   d. sympathized with Southern conservatives.

3. A significant reason that the Medicare proposal was able to overcome opposition and win congressional approval was because it:
   a. made benefits available to all elderly Americans, regardless of need.
   b. strictly regulated the fee structure of doctors and hospitals.
   c. established annual spending ceilings.
   d. shifted responsibility for paying a large proportion of medical fees from the government to the patient.

4. Passed partly in response to events surrounding a demonstration in Selma, Alabama, the Civil Rights Act of 1965 granted blacks:
   a. equal employment opportunities.
   b. access to higher education.
   c. federal protection of their voting rights.
   d. integration in public accommodations.

5. In response to urban racial violence, in 1968 the Commission on Civil Disorders appointed by the president recommended:
   a. massive spending to eliminate the abysmal conditions in the ghettoes.
   b. the elimination of state government involvement in welfare programs.
   c. slowing the pace of racial change to allow the nation a "cooling-off" period.
   d. a return to segregated housing patterns to lessen the emotional conflicts that sparked outbreaks in mixed neighborhoods.

6. The first major race riot of the mid-1960s occurred in the Watts section of:
   a. New York City.
   b. Los Angeles.
   c. Chicago.
   d. Detroit.
   e. Atlanta.

7. The most important and lasting impact of the "black power" movement was the:
   a. stress on the ideal of interracial cooperation.
   b. unification of black political groups.
   c. instilling of racial pride in black Americans.
   d. rejection of African ties and roots by American blacks.

8. Kennedy's "Alliance for Progress" was intended to provide:
   a. mutual reduction of missiles by the United States and the Soviet Union.
   b. additional aid to the Diem government of South Vietnam.
   c. young American volunteers to work in developing nations.
   d. better relations between the United States and Latin America.

9. In the aftermath of the Cuban missile crisis:
   a. Kennedy traveled to Vienna for his first meeting with Soviet Premier Nikita Khrushchev.
   b. the Soviets ordered construction of the Berlin Wall to stop the exodus of East Germans.
   c. a large CIA-trained army of anti-Castro Cubans unsuccessfully invaded the island.
   d. both the United States and the Soviet Union seemed ready to move toward a new accommodation.

10. Ngo Dinh Diem turned out to be an unfortunate choice as the basis of American hopes for a noncommunist South Vietnam because by the early 1960s he:
    a. resisted serious political or economic reforms.
    b. failed to attract the support of the Vietnamese upper class.
    c. was too willing to appease the Viet Cong.
    d. persecuted the nation's Roman Catholics.

11. In regard to the Vietnam conflict, the Gulf of Tonkin Resolution:
    a. aroused strong opposition and a lengthy debate in Congress before being narrowly passed.
    b. limited President Johnson to a one-time retaliatory bombing strike on North Vietnam.
    c. was claimed by President Johnson as legal authorization for the military escalation of the U.S. role in the conflict.
    d. marked the beginning of significant international support for the American response to communist aggression in Indochina.

12. By the end of 1967, United States war efforts in Vietnam:
    a. had effectively reduced to a trickle the flow of communist soldiers and supplies into the south part of Vietnam by intensive bombings of the north.
    b. involved nearly 500,000 American military personnel in the war region.
    c. had succeeded in establishing an honest and efficient, if weak, government in South Vietnam.
    d. All of the above

13. The American military in Vietnam seemed *least* capable of:
    a. winning a military victory in the major battles in which it became engaged.
    b. removing the Viet Cong and their Vietnamese allies from the north from such strongholds as Khesanh.
    c. sustaining a "favorable kill ratio."
    d. pacifying a captured region by winning the "hearts and minds" of the people.

14. The Tet offensive by Viet Cong forces in January 1968 was most significant because it demonstrated:
    a. a display of military strength by the Viet Cong that American commanders had long insisted that the Viet Cong did not possess.
    b. that American forces had the military might to dislodge the Viet Cong from most of the positions that they had seized during the previous three years.
    c. that Saigon was a safe haven for international diplomats and businessmen despite the problems in the rest of the country.
    d. that the vast majority of the American public would increase their support for the war effort in the wake of U.S. military victories.

15. In the 1968 presidential election, George Wallace enjoyed an unusually high degree of support for a third-party candidate because he argued that:
    a. the United States should not have any military involvement in Vietnam.
    b. the movement toward racial equality should be accelerated through "affirmative action" programs.
    c. programs to alleviate poverty should be fully funded by Congress and that defense spending should be cut sharply to get the money.
    d. busing for racial integration, expanding government regulations and social programs, and soft treatment of rioters and demonstrators were destroying America.

True/False

Read each statement carefully. Mark true statements "T" and false statements "F."

___1. Because it promised another round of reform like the New Deal, the nickname given to President Kennedy's agenda for social reform was the "Kennedy Round."

___2. The Warren Commission on the assassination of president Kennedy concluded that Lee Harvey Oswald had acted alone.

___3. Barry Goldwater, the Republican nominee for president in 1964, represented the moderate-liberal wing of his party, and his defeat laid the groundwork for the conservative takeover of the Republican Party that would follow.

___4. The Office of Economic Opportunity (OEO), the "centerpiece" of President Johnson's "war on poverty," tried to get members of poor communities themselves involved in planning and administering social programs.

___5. The Immigration Act of 1965 gave preference to potential northern and western European migrants and sharply limited African and Asian immigration to the United States.

___6. A major key to President Johnson's "Great Society" was that the programs involved reform in the approach to poverty without necessitating significant spending increases.

___7. In the immediate post–World War II period, there was a major exodus of black population from the industrial cities of the Northeast back to the South because of urban riots and the loss of wartime jobs.

___8. By the mid-1960s the civil rights movement had begun to focus on racial discrimination that existed by custom and practice outside the South as well as on legal restrictions in the old Confederate states.

___9. "Affirmative action" refers to extra efforts—for example, hiring, scholarships, etc.—undertaken by the government and corporations to help counter the discrimination that women and minorities faced in the past.

___10. Malcolm X stressed that blacks should band together and stress their racial pride through their Christian churches.

___11. The Green Berets were special forces trained to fight guerrilla conflicts and other limited wars.

___12. Despite pleas for help from anti-Castro exiles, the preparation for the Bay of Pigs invasion was undertaken by Cuban refugees without assistance from any agency of the U.S. government.

___13. The Gulf of Tonkin Resolution, which authorized President Johnson to "take all necessary measures" to protect American forces and "prevent further aggression" in Southeast Asia, was inspired by an alleged attack on U.S. destroyers by North Vietnamese torpedo boats.

___14. The Tet offensive by the Viet Cong helped turn American opinion against the war in Vietnam even though the U.S. and South Vietnamese forces repelled the invasion and inflicted serious losses on the Viet Cong.

___15. Despite Martin Luther King, Jr.'s philosophy of nonviolence, there were major riots in several American cities following the assassination of King.

Review Questions

These questions are to be answered with essays. This will allow you to explore relationships among individuals, events, and attitudes of the period under review.

1. What were the central elements of the New Frontier and the Great Society? Why was Johnson able to succeed where Kennedy failed? What were the long-term results of the liberal legislation of 1964 to 1966?

2. How did the reaction of many southern whites to the civil rights activities ironically serve to help the blacks' cause? How did blacks respond when it became clear that the legislative victories of 1964 and 1965 were not enough to satisfy their aspirations?

3. What was the heart of the problem in Vietnam that made military victory so difficult, if not impossible? Who seemed to understand this problem better—the Johnson administration or its critics? How was the Johnson administration trapped by the war?

CHAPTER THIRTY-TWO

The Crisis of Authority

OBJECTIVES

A thorough study of Chapter 32 should enable you to understand:
1. The reasons for the rise of the New Left and the counterculture.
2. The problems of American Indians and Hispanics, and the nature of their protest movements.
3. The meaning of the new feminism.
4. The Nixon-Kissinger policy for terminating the Vietnam War, and the subsequent Paris peace settlement.
5. The changes in American foreign policy necessitated by the new perception of the world as multipolar.
6. The ways in which the Supreme Court in the Nixon years began a change to a more conservative posture, and the reasons for this change.
7. The reasons for the decline in the American economy in the early 1970s, and President Nixon's reaction to the decline.
8. The significance of Watergate as an indication of the abuse of executive power.

PERTINENT QUESTIONS

The Youth Culture (pp. 945–951)

1. What led to the rise of the New Left? How did the Vietnam War and the draft inflame the movement? What were its results?
2. What were the main manifestations of the counterculture of the 1960s? What role did drugs play? To what extent was it "an exaggerated expression of impulses that were coursing through the larger society?
3. What did the Woodstock and Altamont music festivals reveal about the positive and negative sides of the youth culture of the 1960s?

The Mobilization of Minorities (pp. 951–956)

4. How did the Indian civil rights movement manifest itself? What changes did it accomplish?
5. Describe the typical economic status of Hispanic Americans. What organizational efforts did they undertake to improve conditions?
6. What were the accomplishments of the gay liberation movement? What resistance did it face?

The New Feminism (pp. 956–960)

7. What were the goals of the National Organization for Women?
8. How did the women's movement evolve, and how did the most radical positions taken by feminists differ from more mainstream positions?
9. What gains did women make in education, the professions, and politics in the 1970s and 1980s?
10. What happened to the Equal Rights Amendment? Why?
11. What brought the abortion controversy to the front burner of American politics in the 1970s?

Nixon, Kissinger, and the War (pp. 960–964)

12. Explain Richard Nixon's "Vietnamization" policy. How well did it work? Why did it defuse some of the opposition to the war?
13. What direction did the antiwar movement take in reaction to the invasion of Cambodia?
14. What did the Pentagon Papers reveal about the nature of the Vietnam War?
15. What effect did the controversial and inconclusive nature of the war have on the military personnel who served in Vietnam?
16. What did the bombings and negotiations from March 1972 to January 1973 accomplish? What role did the U.S. presidential election campaign play in shaping the nation's understanding of the progress of the negotiations?
17. What were the main provisions of the Paris accords? How did they fall apart?
18. On balance, what were the costs of the war to Vietnam and the United States?

Nixon, Kissinger, and the World (pp. 964–967)

19. Why did Nixon and Henry Kissinger decide that the time had come for rapprochement with China? What resulted from Nixon's visit and related initiatives? Why was his handshake with Chou En-lai so symbolic?

20. What was the basic thrust of the Nixon Doctrine? What were its implications in Chile?

21. What dilemma of American policy in the Middle East did the Yom Kippur War make clear? What other lessons did the war teach?

Politics and Economics in the Nixon Years (pp. 968–973)

22. To what extent was Nixon's domestic policy a mix of conservative reaction to the Great Society and new progressive proposals?

23. What major decisions of the Warren Court most outraged conservatives? What successes and rebuffs did Nixon meet in his attempts to reshape the Supreme Court?

24. What advantages did Nixon have going into the 1972 election? What were George McGovern's political liabilities?

25. What were the proximate and fundamental causes of the inflation problem of the late 1960s and 1970s?

26. Explain how the nation's manufacturing sector and, therefore, the nature of the economy was changing. How did corporate America respond?

27. Describe the general outlines of Nixon's economic policy. Was it consistent? Was it effective?

The Watergate Crisis (pp. 973–978)

28. What aspects of Richard Nixon's personality and management style led to the collection of scandals associated with the Watergate crisis?

29. Why did Spiro Agnew resign? Why did his removal and the appointment of Gerald Ford as vice president actually increase the pressure on Nixon?

30. On what charges would Nixon's probable impeachment and conviction have been based? Why did he finally resign?

IDENTIFICATION

Identify each of the following, and explain why it is important within the context of the chapter.

1. Students for a Democratic Society (SDS)
2. hippies
3. LSD
4. the Beatles
5. American Indian Movement (AIM)
6. Indian Civil Rights Act
7. César Chávez
8. "Stonewall Riot"
9. Betty Friedan
10. Sandra Day O'Connor
11. Geraldine Ferraro
12. *Roe* v. *Wade*
13. Henry Kissinger
14. My Lai massacre
15. prisoners of war
16. Ho Chi Minh City
17. Khmer Rouge
18. "bipolar" and "multipolar"
19. SALT I
20. Leonid Brezhnev
21. "silent majority"
22. *Miranda* v. *Arizona*
23. Warren Burger
24. George Wallace
25. Organization of Petroleum Exporting Countries (OPEC)
26. "stagflation"
27. Gerald Ford

DOCUMENT

Read the text section entitled "The Watergate Crisis" (p. 973). All along, President Nixon had claimed that neither he nor any of his inner staff knew any of the details of the Watergate break-in. He also denied that he had been involved in any cover-up. Through July 1974, the evidence against Nixon was circumstantial or based on contradictory testimony. Although the pressure for removal at that time was strong, the president still had many defenders. Then in August, Nixon was forced to release the tapes that are excerpted below. They cover conversations of June 23, 1972, only six days after the break-in. Read the excerpts, and consider these questions: Were these tapes necessary for Nixon's impeachment, or was there adequate evidence without them? What do the conversations reveal about the casual manner in which Nixon and White House assistant H. R. Haldeman used federal agencies for political purposes?

HALDEMAN: Now, on the investigation, you know the Democratic break-in thing, we're back in the problem area because the FBI is not under control because Gray [Patrick Gray, acting director of the FBI] doesn't exactly know how to control it and they have—their investigation is now leading into some productive areas—because they've been able to trace the money—not through the money itself—but through the bank sources—the banker. And it goes in some directions we don't want it to go. . . . That the way to handle this now is for us to have Walters [General Vernon Walters, deputy director of the CIA] call Pat Gray and just say, "Stay to hell out of this—this is ah, business here we don't want you to go any further on it." That's not an unusual development, and ah, that would take care of it. . . .

NIXON: Well, what the hell, did Mitchell [John Mitchell, former attorney general and head of the president's campaign] know about this?

HALDEMAN: I think so. I don't think he knew the details, but I think he knew.

HALDEMAN (about three hours later): Well, it was kind of interesting. Walters made the point and I didn't mention Hunt [E. Howard Hunt, ex-CIA agent and White House consultant who was convicted in the Watergate conspiracy]. I just said that the thing was leading into directions that were going to create potential problems because they were exploring leads that led back into areas that would be harmful to the CIA and harmful to the government. . . .

Recorded presidential conversation submitted to the Committee on the Judiciary of the House of Representatives by Richard Nixon, April 30, 1974.

MAP EXERCISE

Fill in or identify the following on the blank map provided. You will need to consult an atlas to complete these exercises.

1. Identify and label the following countries: China (mainland), China (Taiwan), Japan, North Korea, South Korea, Soviet Union, and Vietnam.
2. Identify and label the location of Beijing.

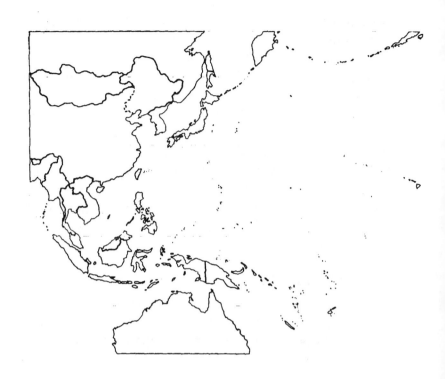

Interpretative Questions

Based on what you have filled in, answer the following. For some of the questions you will need to consult the narrative in your text for information or explanation.

1. How realistic was it for the United States to regard the government on Taiwan as the legitimate government of mainland China?

2. Describe the strategic geographic position of mainland China. How was this a factor in making renewed relations with China important to the United States?

SUMMARY

Opposition to the war in Vietnam became the centerpiece of a wide-ranging political and cultural challenge to traditional American society. During this turbulent era, African Americans, women, Hispanics, and Indians organized to assert their rights. Richard Nixon inherited the war in Vietnam, and he did bring it to an end. The cost of Nixon's four years of war was thousands of Americans lives and many more thousands of

Asian lives, plus continued social unrest at home and an enduring strain on the economy. The end of American involvement did not mean that the goal of an independent, noncommunist South Vietnam had been secured. Nixon was more successful in his other foreign policy initiatives, opening meaningful contacts with China and somewhat easing tensions with the Soviet Union. He managed to stake out a solid constituency of conservative voters with his attacks on liberal programs and ideas. He never quite decided how to deal with a troubled and changing economy that faced the unusual dual problems of slowed growth and rapidly rising prices. Less than two years after his overwhelming reelection in 1972, Nixon resigned from office under fire from a nation horrified by his arrogant misuse of presidential power for personal political purposes in the Watergate affair.

CHAPTER SELF-TEST

After you have read the chapter in the text and done the exercises in the study guide, the following self-test can be taken to see if you understand the material you have covered. Answers appear at the end of the study guide.

Multiple Choice

Circle the letter of the response that best answers the question or completes the statement.

1. Although the philosophy of the counterculture seemed to favor all of the following, the characteristic that most defined the movement was:
   a. rejecting the inhibitions and conventions of middle-class culture and concentrating on pleasure and fulfillment.
   b. striving for racial and social justice for all peoples.
   c. breaking the power of corrupt elites who controlled American corporations and governments.
   d. demanding an end to international wars and conflicts and substituting peaceful resolution.

2. Compared to the national population, Native Americans by the 1960s had a much higher level of:
   a. family income.
   b. educational attainment.
   c. life expectancy.
   d. joblessness.

3. By the 1980s, Hispanic Americans had:
   a. become the fastest-growing minority group in the nation.
   b. yet to make any efforts to organize themselves politically or economically.
   c. strenuously opposed the concept of bilingualism in education.
   d. consistently championed the ideal of the "melting pot."

4. In *The Feminine Mystique* (1963), Betty Friedan:
   a. praised and endorsed the ideal of women living happy, fulfilled lives in purely domestic roles.
   b. discovered that many of the college-educated women in her study were deeply frustrated and unhappy, with no outlets for their intelligence, talent, and education.
   c. called for women to band together to launch an all-out assault on the male power structure.
   d. rejected the whole notion of marriage, family, and heterosexual intercourse.

5. According to most historians, a major reason that the Equal Rights Amendment (ERA) failed to gain ratification was:
   a. widespread public apathy and indifference about the issue.
   b. lack of time for proper organization of support groups to push for ratification in the states.
   c. fears by many Americans that it would create a major disruption of traditional social patterns.
   d. inadequate evidence of actual instances of political and economic discrimination toward women.

6. Nixon's policy of "Vietnamization" succeeded in:
   a. increasing the number of American military recruits.
   b. helping temporarily to quiet domestic opposition to the war.
   c. breaking the stalemate in the negotiations with the North Vietnamese.
   d. reducing the role of the White House in conduct of the war.

7. Public clamor against the Vietnam War spread in 1971 after the Supreme Court:
   a. ordered the abolition of the Selective Service System.
   b. declared the Gulf of Tonkin Resolution unconstitutional.
   c. ruled that the press had the right to publish the so-called Pentagon Papers.
   d. overturned the war crimes conviction of Lieutenant William Calley.

8. Nixon's plan for "peace with honor" in Vietnam produced a North Vietnamese promise to:
   a. release American prisoners of war.
   b. never again invade the south part of Vietnam.
   c. grant democratic rule to the government in Saigon.
   d. sever its ties with the Soviet Union.
   e. do *none* of the things listed above.

9. In response to a new military offensive against the south by the Vietnamese from the north in March 1975, the United States Congress:
   a. authorized President Ford to renew bombing strikes on both the northern part of Vietnam and on Cambodia.
   b. ordered an immediate withdrawal of all remaining U.S. troops.
   c. organized a rapid and orderly evacuation of American officials from Saigon and the southern part of Vietnam.
   d. refused additional funding for military support of the government in the south of Vietnam.

10. In forging a new relationship with the Chinese communists, the Nixon administration agreed to:
   a. back China in any border disputes with the Soviet Union.
   b. drop its opposition to the admission of communist China to the United Nations.
   c. immediately establish formal diplomatic relations between the United States and China.
   d. begin planning the transition of Taiwan to mainland rule by 1999.

11. The surprise attack Egyptian and Syrian forces launched against Israel marked the start of the:
   a. 1948 War of Independence.
   b. Sinai Conflict of 1956.
   c. Six-Day War of 1967.
   d. Yom Kippur War of 1973.
   e. Suez Crisis of 1979.

12. The Family Assistance Plan, proposed by the Nixon administration, proposed to overhaul the nation's large and cumbersome welfare system by:
   a. providing a minimum guaranteed annual income for all Americans.
   b. granting greater authority for the federal government in guarding against welfare fraud.
   c. establishing a distribution of welfare funds based solely on personal need.
   d. ending cash assistance in favor of an entirely "in kind" system that would provide food, medical care, clothing, rent vouchers, etc., that the poor could not waste.

13. Conservatives were disappointed by the *Roe* v. *Wade* (1972) decision of the Supreme Court, which:
   a. ruled in favor of the use of forced busing to achieve racial balance in schools.
   b. overturned existing statutes providing for capital punishment.
   c. clearly established the right of individuals to keep pornographic materials in the privacy of their homes.
   d. upheld the principle of affirmative action.
   e. struck down laws forbidding women to choose to have abortions.

14. All of the following factors contributed to Richard M. Nixon's overwhelming reelection in 1972 *except* the:
   a. seemingly successful negotiations moving toward an end to the war in Vietnam.
   b. acknowledged honesty and integrity of his campaign workers.
   c. disarray and confusion in the Democratic Party.
   d. withdrawal of candidate George Wallace following his being seriously wounded in an assassination attempt.

15. Tapes of recorded conversations about the Watergate incident ultimately provided convincing evidence that President Nixon had:
   a. no personal connection with or knowledge of the efforts to cover up his campaign's involvement in the incident.
   b. actually planned the details of the break-in at the Democratic National Committee's office.
   c. clear knowledge that actions were being undertaken to distance his campaign staff from all appearance of involvement with Watergate.
   d. tried to blame the event on the Democrats themselves.

True/False

Read each statement carefully. Mark true statements "T" and false statements "F."

___1.   The New Left movement drew strength from the civil rights and anti-Vietnam War mood of many Americans.

___2.   The counterculture movement and the "hippies" of the 1960s had very little impact on the overt behavior of broader society.

___3.   The avowed goal of the American Indian movement was to break down tribal allegiance and encourage Native Americans to assimilate into the mainstream of middle-class values.

___4.   A major result of the gay liberation movement was that homosexuals became more willing to make their sexual preference known publicly and unapologetically.

___5.   Betty Friedan's 1963 book *The Feminine Mystique* helped launch the women's liberation movement by showing that many college-educated women were frustrated by their limited opportunities.

___6.   The Equal Rights Amendment (ERA) became part of the U.S. Constitution in 1972 when Georgia became the thirty-eighth state to ratify it.

___7.   The *Roe* v. *Wade* decision of the U.S. Supreme Court used the "right to privacy" as the basis for ruling that states could not ban all abortions.

___8.   President Nixon's policy of "Vietnamization" involved an effort to get the South Vietnamese military to take an increasingly large portion of the burden of combat so that the United States could reduce its ground forces involved in the war.

___9.   The outpouring of patriotism that accompanied the invasion of Cambodia by U.S. troops in 1970 temporarily quieted the anti-Vietnam War protest movement.

___10.   The Department of Defense documents released in the so-called Pentagon Papers revealed that the U.S. government had been less than fully honest in reporting to the American people about the military progress of the war.

___11.   According to President Nixon, the "Christmas bombings" of 1972 forced the North Vietnamese to agree to a cease-fire.

___12.   Henry Kissinger convinced Richard Nixon to take a bipolar vision of the world in which the United States stood essentially alone against communism everywhere it surfaced.

___13. Although President Nixon began the process of opening up U.S. contact with mainland China, he was not willing to allow the mainland government to replace Taiwan in the United Nations and on the Security Council.

___14. The Nixon administration faced the problem of dealing with the inflationary pressures caused by an ever-increasing proportion of the American work force being employed in high-paid, skilled jobs in manufacturing.

___15. Using the justification of protecting "national security," President Nixon fostered an attitude in the members of his administration that led to efforts to stifle dissent and undermine political opposition.

Review Questions

These questions are to be answered with essays. This will allow you to explore relationships among individuals, events, and attitudes of the period under review.

1. Chronicle the several cultural and ethnic movements that arose in the 1960s and early 1970s to challenge traditional white, male-dominated society. How did more conservative forces respond? How extensive and lasting were the changes?

2. What was accomplished during the four years that the Nixon administration carried on the war in Vietnam? Could the peace have been achieved in a better manner at less human cost?

3. What were the several assumptions reflected in Nixon and Kissinger's rapprochement with the Soviet Union and China? Were the assumptions valid and the actions wise?

4. Was the Watergate scandal mainly a product of the changing institution of the presidency and the domestic crises presented by the Cold War and Vietnam, as some historians aruge, or was it, as others maintain, rooted "in the personality and history of Nixon himself"?

CHAPTER THIRTY-THREE
The "Age of Limits"

OBJECTIVES

A thorough study of Chapter 33 should enable you to understand:

1. The efforts of President Gerald Ford to overcome the effects of Richard Nixon's resignation.
2. The rapid emergence of Jimmy Carter as a national figure and the reasons for his victory in 1976.
3. Carter's emphasis on human rights and its effects on international relations.
4. Carter's role in bringing about the Camp David agreement and the impact of this agreement on the Middle East.
5. Why the United States had so much difficulty in freeing the hostages held by Iran and the effect of this episode on the Carter presidency.
6. The political importance of the rise of the Sunbelt and the increasing strength of conservative, evangelical Christianity.
7. The nature of the "Reagan revolution" and the meaning of "supply-side" economics.
8. The staunchly anticommunist Reagan foreign policy.

PERTINENT QUESTIONS

Politics and Diplomacy After Watergate (pp. 981–988)

1. How did his pardon of Richard Nixon affect Gerald Ford's political standing?
2. What economic challenges did Ford face? How did he respond?
3. How did Jimmy Carter's background and personality shape the tone of his presidency and people's reaction to him?
4. What economic and energy-related problems did Carter face?
5. What general principle formed the basis of Carter's approach to foreign policy?

6. How did Carter manage to help bring about a peace treaty between Egypt and Israel? Why was it "the crowning achievement of his presidency"?

7. What led to the Iranian hostage crisis? What political effects did it have on the Carter administration? How was the crisis resolved?

8. How did the Carter administration react to the Soviet invasion of Afghanistan?

The Rise of the American Right (pp. 989–994)

9. Where is the "Sunbelt"? What were the political implications of its rise?

10. Describe the basis of Christian Evangelicalism. How could it lead to both social liberalism, as in Jimmy Carter, and cultural conservatism, as in Jerry Falwell?

11. What were the elements of the New Right movement? How did it come to have such influence in the Republican Party?

12. To what extent was the tax revolt of the 1970s and 1980s as much an attack on government programs as on taxes? How did the tax cut activists avoid specific confrontations with supporters of key programs?

13. Why did Ronald Reagan win such a decisive victory in 1980? What happened in the congressional races?

The "Reagan Revolution" (pp. 994–1000)

14. What personal factors helped make Reagan politically effective? Why was he called the "Teflon president"?

15. Explain the assumptions made by "supply-side" economists ("Reaganomics") and how the Reagan administration implemented supply-side policies. How did the economy respond to the administration's policy?

16. What led to the enormous budget deficits and fiscal crisis of the mid-1980s? How effective was the Reagan administration's effort to reduce the deficit?

17. What stance toward the Soviets and communism in general constituted the so-called Reagan Doctrine? How did the doctrine play out in Grenada and elsewhere in Latin America?

18. How did the Reagan administration's reaction to the 1983 barracks bombing in Beirut reveal restraint in the face of Middle Eastern terrorism?

19. Was the election of 1984 more a personal victory for Ronald Reagan or the mark of a new Republican era?

IDENTIFICATION

Identify each of the following, and explain why it is important within the context of the chapter.

1. Henry Kissinger
2. SALT II
3. Panama Canal Treaty
4. Camp David accords
5. Diplomatic relations with China
6. Ayatollah Ruhollah Khomeini
7. Sagebrush Rebellion
8. "born again"
9. Moral Majority
10. Pat Robertson
11. Nelson Rockefeller
12. Proposition 13
13. Edward Kennedy
14. OPEC
15. "entitlement" programs
16. Gramm-Rudman-Hollings Act
17. Strategic Defense Initiative ("Star Wars")
18. "Sandinistas"
19. Palestinian Liberation Organization (PLO)
20. Walter Mondale
21. Geraldine Ferraro

DOCUMENT

Read the text sections entitled "The Trials of Jimmy Carter" (p. 984) and "The Reagan Revolution" (p. 994), paying attention to the differing styles and personalities of the two presidents. The excerpts below, the first from Carter's so-called malaise speech of July 15, 1979, and the second from Reagan's State of the Union Address on February 4, 1986, illustrate their contrasting styles. Carter's address was given at a time when he was under considerable attack for his leadership, whereas Reagan's was delivered while his popularity was at its height. Both speeches contained specific legislative agendas, but they are more memorable for their general messages than for their specific proposals. Consider the following questions: How do the two documents illustrate the differences between the leadership styles of Reagan and Carter? Each speech cited experiences or opinions of supposedly typical Americans;

compare and contrast the use of these examples. The America described by Reagan in 1986 was very different from that described by Carter in 1979; had America truly changed that much? Had Reagan restored national confidence through rhetoric or through long-term solutions to difficult problems? In light of the state of the nation and the world in the early 1990s, which speech was more realistic? Which was more prophetic?

JIMMY CARTER, JULY 15, 1979

Ten days ago I had plans to speak to you again about a very important subject—energy. For the fifth time I would have described the urgency of the problem and laid out a series of legislative recommendations to the Congress, but as I was preparing to speak I began to ask myself the same question that I know has been troubling many of you: Why have we not been able to get together as a nation to resolve our serious energy crisis?

It's clear that the true problems of our nation are much deeper—deeper than gasoline lines or energy shortages. Deeper, even, than inflation or recession. And I realize more than ever that as President I need your help, so I decided to reach out and listen to the voices of America . . . and I want to share with you what I heard. . . .

Many people talked about themselves and about the conditions of our nation. This from a young woman in Pennsylvania: "I feel so far from government. I feel like ordinary people are excluded from political power." And this from a young Chicano: "Some of us have suffered from recession all our lives." . . .

This kind of summarized a lot of other statements: "Mr. President, we are confronted with a moral and a spiritual crisis." . . .

These 10 days confirmed my belief in the decency and the strength and the wisdom of the American people, but it also bore out some of my long-standing concerns about our nation's underlying problems. . . .

So I want to speak to you tonight about a subject even more serious than energy or inflation. I want to talk to you right now about a fundamental threat to American democracy.

I do not mean our political and civil liberties. They will endure. And I do not refer to the outward strength of America—the nation that is at peace tonight everywhere in the world with unmatched economic power and military might. The threat is nearly invisible in ordinary ways. It is a crisis of confidence. It is a crisis that strikes at the very heart and soul and spirit of our national will.

We can see this crisis in the growing doubt about the meaning of our own lives and in the loss of a unity of purpose for our nation.

The erosion of our confidence in the future is threatening to destroy the social and the political fabric of America. The confidence that we have always had as a people is not simply some romantic dream or a proverb in a dusty book that we read just on the Fourth of July. It is the idea which rounded our nation and which has guided our development as a people. Confidence in the future has supported everything else—public institutions and private enterprise, our own families and the very Constitution of the United States. Confidence has defined our course and has served as a link between generations.

We've always believed in something called progress. We've always had a faith that the days of our children would be better than our own.

Our people are losing that faith. . . .But just as we are losing our confidence in the future, we are also beginning to close the door on our past.

In a nation that was proud of hard work, strong families, close-knit communities and our faith in God, too many of us now tend to worship self-indulgence and consumption. Human identity is no longer defined by what one does but by what one owns. . . .

Often you see paralysis and stagnation and drift. You don't like it. And neither do I.

What can we do? First of all, we must face the truth and then we can change our course. We simply must have faith in each other. Faith in our ability to govern ourselves and faith in the future of this nation. Restoring that faith and that confidence to America is now the most important task we face. . . .

And we are the generation that will win the war on the energy problem, and in that process rebuild the unity and confidence of America. . . .

Energy will be the immediate test of our ability to unite this nation. And it can also be the standard around which we rally. On the battlefield of energy we can win for our nation a new confidence, and we can seize control again of our common destiny. . . .

[At this point, the speech lists six specific points emphasizing conservation and reduced energy consumption.]

I do not promise you that this struggle for freedom will be easy. I do not promise a quick way out of our nation's problems when the truth is that the only way out is an all-out effort. . . .There is simply no way to avoid sacrifice. . . .

In closing, let me say this: I will do my best, but I will not do it alone. Let your voice be heard. Whenever you have a chance, say something good about our country. With God's help and for the sake of our nation, it is time for us to join hands in America.

Let us commit ourselves together to a rebirth of the American spirit. Working together with our common faith, we cannot fail.

President Jimmy Carter, television address to the nation, July 15, 1979.

RONALD REAGAN, FEBRUARY 4, 1986

I have come to review with you the progress of our nation, to speak of unfinished work and to set our sights on the future. I am pleased to report the state of the union is stronger than a year ago, and growing stronger each day. Tonight, we look out on a rising America—firm of heart, united in spirit, powerful in pride and patriotism. America is on the move.

But it wasn't long ago that we looked out on a different land—locked factory gates, long gasoline lines, intolerable prices and interest rates turning the greatest country on Earth into a land of broken dreams. Government growing beyond our consent had become a lumbering giant, slamming shut the gates of opportunity, threatening to crush the very roots of our freedom.

What brought America back? The American people brought us back—with quiet courage and common sense; the undying faith that in this nation under God the future will be ours, for the future belongs to the free. . . .

Family and community are the co-stars of this great American comeback. They are why we say tonight: private values must be at the heart of public policies.

What is true for families in America is true for America in the family of free nations. History is no captive of some inevitable force. History is made by men and women of vision and courage. Tonight, freedom is on the march. The United States is the economic miracle, the model to which the world once again turns. We stand for an idea whose time is now. . . .

We speak tonight of an agenda for the future, an agenda for a safer, more secure world. And we speak about the necessity for actions to steel us for the challenges of growth, trade, and security in the next decade and the year 2000. And we will do it—not by breaking faith with bedrock principles, but by breaking free from failed policies. . . .

[At this point the speech went into specific proposals for a balanced budget amendment, defense spending, tax reform, and other matters.]

America is ready, America can win the race to the future—and we shall.

The American dream is a song of hope that runs through the night winter air. Vivid, tender music that warms our hearts when the least among us aspire to the greatest things. . . .

The world's hopes rest with America's future. America's hopes rest with us. So let us go forward to create our world of tomorrow—in faith, in unity, and in love. God bless you, and God bless America.

President Ronald Reagan, State of the Union Address, February 4, 1986.

MAP EXERCISE

Fill in or identify the following on the blank map provided. For this exercise you may need to consult an atlas.

1. Circle the USSR-Afghanistan border area.
2. Locate and label the following: Iran, Lebanon, Egypt, Israel.

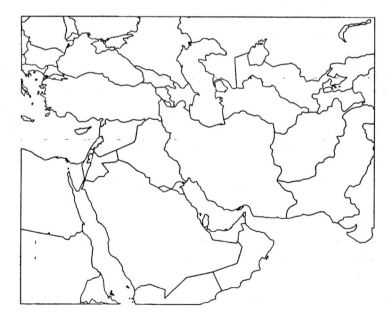

Interpretative Questions

Based on what you have filled in, answer the following. For some of the questions you will need to consult the narrative in your text for information or explanation.

1. Why was the Soviet Union so concerned about the revolution in Afghanistan? Why did the United States support the rebel side?

2. How did the establishment of an apparently lasting peace between Egypt and Israel change the nature of Middle Eastern tension?

3. Why did the United States support the Shah of Iran? Why did his fall present so many problems for America?

SUMMARY

As president, Gerald Ford worked to heal the wounds of Watergate and restore respect for the presidency. His pardon of Richard Nixon was probably the most controversial act of his caretaker period in office. Jimmy Carter turned out to be a more effective campaigner than president. His administration was marked by an inability to set a tone of leadership. He made no significant strides toward solving the energy crisis and took only halting steps toward his goal of making the federal government more efficient. His last year in office was dominated by the Iranian hostage crisis, which at first boosted his popularity but later may have cost him another term. Riding the crest of a wave of his own popularity and new Republican strength from the Sunbelt and conservative Christians, Ronald Reagan won the 1980 election. He exploited deep-seated feelings of resentment over America's seeming weakness abroad and appealed to those who believed that government should play a lesser role in the economy. Congress quickly passed his supply-side economics plan of tax reductions and spending cuts; but a year later, the nation was mired in recession. Prosperity returned and Reagan won easy reelection.

During the 1970s, the age, racial, and regional characteristics of the American population changed. The proportion of the population classified as elderly increased; black and Hispanic figures soared; and the Sunbelt states boomed. Politically, the nation became more conservative, and much of the conservative impetus came from a New Right with strong Protestant evangelical support. Liberals, when they did not back away, shifted their emphasis to environmental issues.

CHAPTER SELF-TEST

After you have read the chapter in the text and done the exercises in the study guide, the following self-test can be taken to see if you understand the material you have covered. Answers appear at the end of the study guide.

Multiple Choice

Circle the letter of the response that best answers the question or completes the statement.

1. In his efforts to curb inflation, President Ford:
   a. initiated temporary price and wage controls.
   b. called for voluntary efforts.
   c. asked for a reduction in interest rates.
   d. urged increased federal spending.

2. Jimmy Carter's success in the election of 1976 resulted partly because:
   a. Ford refused to bow to the Republican right and remove Rockefeller from the ticket.
   b. Carter's considerable service in Washington assured voters of an experienced administrator.
   c. Ford's personality had generated an atmosphere of bitterness and acrimony in Washington.
   d. Carter seemed to possess honesty, piety, and an outsider's skepticism of the federal government.

3. Carter hoped to base American foreign policy on:
   a. flexible military response whenever democratic governments were challenged.
   b. expansion of American economic interests.
   c. retreat from international power and responsibility.
   d. "rollback" of communist influence around the world.
   e. an active dedication to "human rights."

4. In 1979 Jimmy Carter brought two world leaders together at the Camp David presidential retreat and helped negotiate:
   a. a smooth transition of power over Laos from Vietnam to Cambodia.
   b. a peace treaty between Egypt and Israel.
   c. an end to the Arab oil boycott.
   d. the establishment of democratic governments in Nicaragua and El Salvador.

5. The 1979 revolution in Iran resulted from:
   a. the expansion of Soviet influence in the Middle East.
   b. Iranian resentment against the repressive, authoritarian tactics of the American-backed Shah.
   c. Iranian disillusionment with the Ayatollah Ruhollah Khomeini.
   d. a desire by fundamentalist Iranian Muslims to modernize and Westernize their country.

6. The Soviet invasion of Afghanistan in late 1979 was intended by the Soviets to:
   a. overthrow the pro-Western government.
   b. support the activities of Islamic fundamentalists.
   c. settle the conflict between Afghanistan and Pakistan.
   d. keep the existing Marxist government in power.

7. The rapid population growth in the Sunbelt shifted political power to the region and tended to strengthen a political viewpoint that could be characterized as:
   a. conservative, antigovernment.
   b. liberal, government activist.
   c. moderate, middle-of-the-road.
   d. None of the above; the effect was basically neutral.

8. A common thread of evangelical Christianity is a:
   a. belief in personal conversion through direct personal relationship with Jesus.
   b. rejection of modern doctrines of racial equality.
   c. support for "secular humanism."
   d. tendency to avoid applying religious beliefs to political issues.

9. Journalists referred to the Reagan administration as the "Teflon presidency" because:
   a. of its "slick," constantly shifting and inconsistent policies.
   b. blame for problems or mistakes seldom seemed to stick to Reagan himself.
   c. Reagan's style and image failed to attract and retain public support.
   d. the president insisted upon personal planning and direction of day-to-day governmental affairs.

10. According to the theories of "supply-side" economics, the woes of the American economy had resulted from:
    a. inadequate government expenditures.
    b. excessive taxation of private investors.
    c. low interest rates.
    d. tax loopholes that favored the wealthy.

11. A factor that did *not* contribute to the large federal budget deficits of the mid-1980s was:
    a. the escalating costs of "entitlement" programs.
    b. the tax cuts of 1981.
    c. a large increase in military spending.
    d. creation of new social programs to fight poverty.

12. In its conduct of international affairs, the Reagan administration:
    a. denounced the growth of Solidarity, an independent labor organization in Poland.
    b. pursued a policy of détente with the Soviet Union, actively seeking additional arms control agreements.
    c. favored a more active and assertive role for the United States in opposing communism throughout the world.
    d. sought to pressure friendly dictatorship governments to enact internal democratic reforms.

13. President Reagan's Strategic Defense Initiative (SDI), widely known as "Star Wars":
    a. received overwhelming endorsement by the American scientific community.
    b. was proposed as a means of closing the missile gap and enhancing American first-strike capability.
    c. intimidated the Soviets into agreements for further arms reductions.
    d. was designed to intercept ICBMs.

14. Over 200 United States Marines were killed in 1983 when:
    a. Soviet forces shot down a Korean airliner that had strayed into their air space.
    b. Reagan ordered increased military support for the "contras," a Nicaraguan guerrilla movement.
    c. marines were serving as a peacekeeping force in Beirut, Lebanon.
    d. Libyan leader Muammar al-Qaddafi ordered terrorist attacks on U.S. forces in the Mediterranean Sea.

15. Republican victory in the presidential election of 1984 seemed to indicate:
    a. a major realignment of partisan loyalties in the United States.
    b. that the Republican Party could keep control of the U.S. Senate as long as Ronald Reagan headed the ticket.
    c. a major resurgence in interest and voter turnout among American voters.
    d. that the victory was mainly a personal triumph for Ronald Reagan rather than a major across-the-board victory for Republicans.

True/False

Read each statement carefully. Mark true statements "T" and false statements "F."

___1. Gerald Ford's compassionate pardon of Richard Nixon for his role in the Watergate scandal improved Ford's standing in public opinion polls.

___2. President Ford faced the dual problems of inflation and recession.

___3. Ronald Reagan, representing the conservative wing of the Republican Party, challenged President Ford for the Republican nomination in 1976.

___4. In his campaign for president, Jimmy Carter emphasized that he was a Washington "insider" who could be more effective with Congress than President Ford had been.

___5. Jimmy Carter pledged that a major focus of his foreign policy would be the defense of "human rights."

___6. Jimmy Carter canceled U.S. participation in the 1980 summer Olympics in Moscow in protest of the Soviet invasion of Afghanistan.

___7. Jimmy Carter's most politically damaging defeat in Congress was the Senate's refusal to ratify the controversial Panama Canal Treaty.

___8. The Americans being held hostage in Iran were captured in a failed CIA attempt to overthrow the government of Ayatollah Ruhollah Khomeini.

___9. The so-called Sagebrush Rebellion was an effort by liberal Democrats from the western states to replace Jimmy Carter as the party's nominee in 1980.

___10. The term "born again" Christians was used to refer to the large number of individuals who strayed away from the church during the turbulent 1960s but who returned to regular church attendance in their 1970s and 1980s.

___11. The so-called tax revolt of the late 1970s emerged because there was widespread agreement on the list of government programs that needed to be cut back.

___12. Although Ronald Reagan was not able to fulfill his promise to balance the federal budget, he was able to reverse the trend of the Carter years and reduce the total annual deficit.

___13. The invasion of Grenada by U.S. Marines was an example of the "Reagan Doctrine" that called for U.S. intervention to support opponents of communism.

___14. The Soviet Union favored Reagan's Strategic Defense Initiative ("Star Wars") because it would relieve their economy of the burden of financing a continued arms race.

___15. In 1984 the Democrats nominated a female as Walter Mondale's vice presidential running mate.

Review Questions

These questions are to be answered with essays. This will allow you to explore relationships among individuals, events, and attitudes of the period under review.

1. Did Gerald Ford's pardon of Richard Nixon accomplish its purpose to "shut and seal the book" on Watergate? What else did Ford do to try to restore credibility to the presidency?

2. How effective was Jimmy Carter in applying the human-rights principle to American foreign policy? How did his approach differ from the actions taken by Ronald Reagan?

3. How did the nation's energy needs complicate both the foreign and domestic policies of presidents Ford, Carter, and Reagan?

4. Why was Ronald Reagan so popular despite the ineffectiveness of many of his policies—especially with regard to the budget deficit?

5. How did the shift away from a bipolar world change the very foundation of American foreign policy as it had been practiced since World War II?

CHAPTER THIRTY-FOUR

Modern Times

OBJECTIVES

A thorough study of Chapter 34 should enable you to understand:

1. How the Cold War came to an end and the reasons for the fall of the Soviet Union.
2. The U.S. response to the end of the Cold War and the disintegration of the Soviet Union.
3. The problems that plagued the last years of the Reagan administration.
4. The Bush administration's response to a changing world and economy.
5. The reasons that Bill Clinton won the presidency and how his centrist approach led to great popularity despite personal scandal.
6. The fundamental changes in the American economy after 1970.
7. The increasingly important role of technology, especially the computer, in American life.
8. The profound demographic changes that the nation experienced from the 1970s into the 1990s and the related challenges of "multiculturalism."
9. The widening gulf between economically successful African Americans and the urban black underclass.
10. The troublesome and divisive issues such as drugs, AIDS, abortion, and environmental threats.

PERTINENT QUESTIONS

America and the Waning of the Cold War (pp. 1002–1012)

1. Describe the process by which the Soviet Bloc and the Soviet Union itself ceased to exist. What emerged in its place?
2. How did Ronald Reagan react to Mikhail Gorbachev? What concrete agreement resulted? How did George Bush build on this relationship?

3. What caused the savings and loan crisis? How did it end?

4. Describe the Iran-contra scandal. What was its political impact?

5. What main campaign strategy did George Bush use to come from behind and defeat Michael Dukakis? What happened in the congressional elections?

6. What budgetary and economic problems dominated domestic concerns during the Bush presidency? How did the budget package in 1990 violate Bush's campaign pledge?

7. Why did the United States invade Panama in 1989? How did this action fit with the general direction of post–Cold War foreign policy?

8. What precipitated the Gulf War? What were the long-term outcomes after the relatively easy victory?

9. Why did Bill Clinton win the presidency in 1992?

Partisan Struggles (pp. 1012–1021)

10. What obstacles to effective leadership did Clinton face upon taking office? Which of the administration's own actions compounded its problems?

11. What major domestic and international trade legislation did the Clinton administration manage to push through in its first year? In what major domestic initiative did the administration fail? Why?

12. What did the Clinton administration accomplish in Bosnia? What new Balkan conflict emerged?

13. What led to the Republican sweep of congressional elections in 1994? What political barriers did the GOP face in trying to get its programs through Congress?

14. How did Bill Clinton turn around his political fortunes between 1994 and 1996 to win reelection?

15. What changes in health care coverage for workers and welfare for the poor did Congress pass in 1996?

16. How did Clinton and Congress work together to produce the first balanced budget in three decades?

17. Explain how the Whitewater investigation merged with charges of sexual misconduct to lead to the impeachment of President Clinton. How did his standing with the public hold up through the long controversy? How did the impeachment trial end? What did the whole episode say about the nature of American politics?

The Global Economy (pp. 1021–1028)

18. What technological advance made possible the personal computer? How did the PC change business processes and even household activities?
19. Describe the rapid rise of the computer and software industry. How did Microsoft come to be so large and dominant?
20. What technological developments made the Internet and the World Wide Web possible? What impact did the new medium of communications have on American life?
21. Describe the rise of genetic engineering and the biotechnology industry. What are the future possibilities in this new field?
22. What is meant by the "two-tiered economy"? What factors contributed to this characteristic of the 1990s? What happened to the poverty rate over the post–World War II era?
23. Describe the "globalization" of the American economy. How was it facilitated by NAFTA and GATT? How did globalization affect industrial workers?

A Changing Society (pp. 1028–1036)

24. Why did the average age of Americans increase? What are the social, political, and economic consequences of this demographic change?
25. Describe the significant change in the nature and extent of immigration to the United States after 1965 What two groups had the most impact?
26. Compare and contrast post-1960s accomplishments of the African-American middle class with those of the underclass. What explains the stark disparity?
27. Describe rap music and hip-hop. How did they reflect the culture of the young urban black male?
28. What precipitated the massive 1992 Los Angeles riot? What broader implications did the event have for American race relations?
29. How did illegal drug use in the 1990s vary between middle-class and poor urban neighborhoods?
30. Describe the AIDS epidemic. How did the pattern of infection change over time? What new medications provided hope for those infected with HIV?
31. What led to the decline in the crime rate in the late 1990s? How did this unexpected development combine with general prosperity to create a sense of national contentment?

32. What were the key arguments on which the "right-to-life" movement rested its opposition to abortion? What gains did the movement make? How did the "pro-choice" forces respond?

33. In addition to "pro-choice," what issues concerned activist women in the 1990s? What issue was brought to the forefront by the Supreme Court confirmation hearings of Judge Clarence Thomas?

34. Describe the shift of the political left to emphasis on environmental concerns. What incidents and issues attracted the most attention?

35. How did modern environmentalists differ from traditional conservationists? What new social ethic and economic approach did the ardent environmentalists propound?

36. Compare and contrast the forces that standardized mass culture with the emerging more targeted or fragmented tendencies. How did new media technologies facilitate segmentation?

37. At its core, what is meant by "multiculturalism" and why did some people resist it? What anniversary highlighted the controversy?

IDENTIFICATION

Identify each of the following, and explain why it is important within the context of the chapter.

1. *glasnost* and *perestroika*
2. Tiananmen Square massacre
3. apartheid
4. Nelson Mandela
5. INF Treaty
6. Oliver North
7. Saddam Hussein
8. Norman Schwartzkopf
9. Hillary Rodham Clinton
10. Ross Perot
11. "Contract with America"
12. Newt Gingrich
13. Robert Dole
14. Monica Lewinsky
15. Kenneth Starr

16. Apple II
17. *The Bell Curve*
18. O. J. Simpson trial
19. Rachel Carson's *Silent Spring*
20. "Earth Day"
21. Environmental Protection Agency
22. ecology

DOCUMENT

Read the text section entitled "The Global Economy" (p. 1021). Trade and technology are among the forces that contribute to making the American economy increasingly two-tiered in nature. Some social commentators have expressed fears that the technological revolution may accentuate the division of the nation into structurally separate haves and have-nots. Many politicians and some economists have expressed fears that U.S. prosperity is threatened by increasing globalization that leads corporations to shift jobs and capital abroad. President Clinton addressed both of these issues not by trying to restrict trade and hold back technology, but by actively promoting both, as indicated in the excerpts from two speeches below. He took up the theme of computer technology in his commencement speech at Massachusetts Institute of Technology in June 1998, and he addressed globalization at the Summit of the Americas in December 1994 in Miami. How accurate are the President's appeals to history that he uses to shape his vision of the future?

[M.I.T., June 1998] I come today not to talk about the new marvels of science and engineering. . . . Instead, I come to MIT, an epicenter of the seismic shifts in our economy and society, to talk about how we can and must apply enduring American values to this revolutionary time—about the responsibilities we all have as citizens to include every American in the promise of this new age. . . . Today, I ask you to focus on the challenges of the Information Age. . . . We can extend opportunity to all Americans or leave many behind. We can erase lines of inequity or etch them indelibly. . . . The tools we develop today are bringing down barriers of race and gender, of income and age. . . . For the very first time in our history, it is now possible for a child in the most isolated inner-city neighborhood or rural community to have access to the same world of knowledge at the same instant as the child in the most affluent suburb. Imagine the revolutionary democratizing potential this can bring. Imagine the enormous benefits to our economy, our society, if not just a fraction, but all young people can master this set of twenty-first-century skills. . . .

Yet today, affluent schools are almost three times as likely to have Internet access in the classroom; white students more than twice as likely as black students to have computers in their homes. We know from hard experience that unequal education hardens into unequal prospects. We know the Information Age will accelerate this trend. . . .

History teaches us that even as new technologies create growth and new opportunity, they can heighten economic inequalities and sharpen social divisions. That is, after all, exactly what happened with the mechanization of agriculture and in the Industrial Revolution. As we move into the Information Age, we have it within our power to avoid these developments. . . . But until every child has a computer in the classroom and a teacher well-trained to help, until every student has the skills to tap the enormous resources of the Internet, until every high-tech company can find skilled workers to fill its high-wage jobs, America will miss the full promise of the Information Age. . . . [At this point President Clinton lays out his plans for funding computers in every school and related educational initiatives.]

All students should feel as comfortable with a keyboard as a chalkboard, as comfortable with a laptop as a textbook. It is critical to ensuring that they all have opportunity in the world of the twenty-first century.

* * *

[Miami, Dec. 1994] . . . the truth is that the United States have never been in a stronger economic position to compete and win in the world. We are also taking bold steps to open new markets and to make the global economy work for our people. For forty years, our markets have been more open than those of many other nations. . . . Just a year ago yesterday, I signed into law NAFTA—the North American Free Trade Agreement. When Congress voted for NAFTA, that even committed the United States to continuing leadership and engagement in the post–Cold War world. . . .

Just yesterday, I signed into law the bill implementing the General Agreement on Tariffs and Trade, the largest agreement ever for free and fair trade. GATT, like NAFTA before it, passed because we had strong bipartisan support in Congress. That is a pattern that must prevail as we continue to pursue open markets and prosperity in this hemisphere and around the world. . . . Once, the United States and its neighbors were clearly divided by seemingly unbridgeable cultural and economic gulfs. But today, superhighways, satellite dishes, and enlightened self-interest draw us together as never before.

MIT Tech Talk, June 10, 1998; and U.S. Dept. of State Dispatch Supplement, May 1995, vol. 6, No. 2, pp. 7–8.

MAP EXERCISE

Fill in or identify the following on the blank map provided. Use an atlas or other reference works as your source.

1. Identify and label the following eastern European nations: Russia, Poland, Hungary, Czechoslovakia, Bulgaria, Romania, Ukraine, and Belarus.
2. Identify and label Germany and Berlin.
3. Mark the old western border of the Soviet Union and shade the nations that were under Soviet dominance during the Cold War.
4. Circle the area of the former Yugoslavia that broke up into smaller republics including Bosnia.
5. Circle the general area of the Gulf War and identify the principal nations involved.

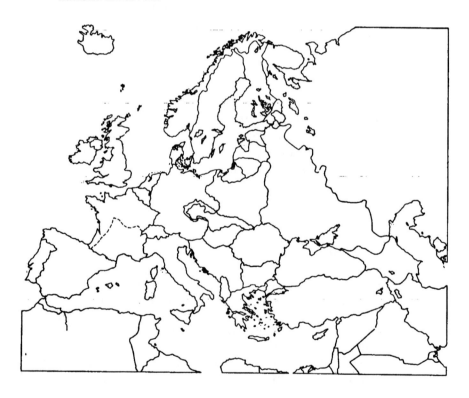

Interpretative Questions

Based on what you have filled in, answer the following. For some of the questions you will need to consult the narrative in your text for information or explanation.

1. Compare and contrast the national borders of Europe before and after the collapse of the Soviet Union and its sphere of influence.
2. Why was having a friendly government in Kuwait so important to the United States and the western European nations?
3. Why were other European nations so concerned about the civil war in Bosnia?

SUMMARY

Although tensions had subsided somewhat, in the early 1980s Americans still thought of the world in the Cold War terms of a communist superpower confronted by the United States and our sometimes difficult allies. The incredible events of 1989 to 1991 saw the end of the Cold War and the demise of the Soviet Union, and the United States was not sure how to react. At home, profound, if more gradual, change was also taking place. America's manufacturing base declined in the face of world competition, economic growth slowed, and poverty began to rise again. Into this mix came a new wave of immigrants dominated not by Europeans but by Asians and Hispanics. As the new century approached, the economy in the age of computers and the Internet had rebounded, medical breakthroughs had reduced the impact of the AIDS epidemic, and crime had declined, but the nation still faced challenges of urban distress, environmental problems, and heightened ethnic and racial tensions.

Republican control of the White House continued with the election of George Bush. The new president faced a very different world situation than had his post–World War II predecessors. The Cold War had ended along with the Soviet Union itself. Bush's popularity soared at the time of the allied victory over Iraq in the Gulf War, but economic problems at home and the other factors led to his defeat in 1992 as Bill Clinton became the first "baby boomer" to be elected president.

CHAPTER SELF-TEST

After you have read the chapter in the text and done the exercises in the study guide, the following self-test can be taken to see if you understand the material you have covered. Answers appear at the end of the study guide.

Multiple Choice

1. The leader of the Soviet Union at the time of the fall of the Berlin Wall and the end of the Cold War was:
   a. Nikita Krushchev.
   b. Boris Yeltsin.
   c. Mikhail Gorbachev.
   d. Leonid Brezhnev.

2. The incident in Tiananmen Square signified that:
   a. communism was dead in Russia.
   b. the eastern European nations were no longer afraid of the Soviet Union.
   c. democracy and human rights would prevail in China.
   d. None of the above

3. "Apartheid" referred to the:
   a. system of racial separation in South Africa.
   b. land ownership patterns in Third World nations that kept peasants poor.
   c. rebirth of ethnic culture and religion in the former satellite nations of the Soviet Union.
   d. the revival of Germany to be the dominant economic force in Europe.

4. The so-called Iran-contra scandal involved the Reagan administration in:
   a. a secret CIA effort to arm Iranian exiles and stage an invasion.
   b. selling weapons to the anti-American government in Iran and using the profit to aid the pro-United States contras in Nicaragua.
   c. planting misleading intelligence information with the governments of Iran and Iraq in order to stir up a war between them.
   d. a scheme to divert frozen Iranian assets into the campaign coffers of a Republican senatorial candidate in Virginia.

5. The Bush administration responded to the alleged drug trafficking by Panamanian military leader Manuel Noriega by:
   a. invading the nation and overthrowing the Noriega government.
   b. imposing an economic boycott on all Panamanian exports.
   c. threatening to close the Panama Canal and deny the Noriega government its share of the tolls.
   d. convincing the Organization of American States to negotiate Noreiga's exile to Chile.

6. Which of the following best describes the Bush administration's approach to the problem of the growing federal budget deficit?
   a. Massive spending cuts proposed by Bush were adopted by Congress, and the deficit declined for the first time since the 1970s.
   b. Despite Bush's "no new taxes" pledge, he worked out a multiyear budget package with Congress that included a significant tax increase.
   c. Congress passed a deficit reduction plan composed of small spending cuts and large tax increases, but Bush vetoed it.
   d. Bush proposed a major tax increase, but conservative Republicans teamed with liberal Democrats to defeat it.

7. A major reason that President Bush's popularity declined rapidly in the months following the end of the Gulf War was that:
   a. he quickly slashed military spending except for the "Star Wars" program.
   b. the Iraqi army reoccupied Kuwait soon after American forces left.
   c. a majority of voters apparently opposed his "pro-choice" position on abortion.
   d. the economy continued in recession and Bush declined to propose policies to combat it.

8. The official United Nations–authorized objective in the Gulf War was to:
   a. remove Saddam Hussein from power in Iraq.
   b. occupy Iraq's oil fields.
   c. reunify Kuwait and Iraq.
   d. expel Iraq's military forces from Kuwait.

9. The general theme stressed most consistently by Bill Clinton in his 1992 presidential campaign was:
   a. the economy.
   b. equal rights for all minorities.
   c. an immediate freeze of military spending.
   d. health-care reform.

10. Hillary Rodham Clinton emerged as an extremely influential first lady whose principal focus in the first year or so of the Clinton administration was on:
    a. mental health.
    b. child welfare.
    c. educational improvements.
    d. health-care reform.

11. The American economy in the period from the late 1980s to the late 1990s was characterized by all of the following *except:*
    a. the lowest rate of poverty since World War II.
    b. a decline in the relative importance of heavy manufacturing.
    c. healthy increases in income for educated Americans, especially in science and engineering.
    d. unequal distribution of wealth and income.

12. From 1965 to the early 1990s there was a significant relative and actual increase in immigration by all of the following groups *except:*
    a. Asians.
    b. Mexicans.
    c. Puerto Ricans.
    d. Europeans.

13. Which of the following best represents the economic status of African Americans by the 1980s?
    a. Despite the efforts of the 1960s all classes of blacks were falling further behind whites.
    b. The black middle class had made significant gains but the gap between the black middle class and underclass had widened.
    c. Working-class blacks made significant strides, but white-collar options remained closed, so middle-class blacks made little gains.
    d. Except in the South, average family income for blacks matched that of whites by the 1990 census.

14. The "Contract with America" was:
    a. a statement of goals by congressional Republicans led by Newt Gingrich.
    b. Bill Clinton's pledge to follow a centrist approach to domestic policy.
    c. the manifesto of the new environmental movement.
    d. the campaign platform of Ross Perot and the Independent Party.

15. The company that emerged most dominant from the PC revolution was:
    a. IBM.
    b. Remington Rand.
    c. Apple.
    d. Microsoft.

True/False

Read each statement carefully. Mark true statements "T" and false statements "F."

___1.   In the reforming Soviet Union, *glasnost* referred to the dismantling of repression and *perestroika* referred to economic restructuring.

___2.   The white South African leader who worked with President Carter to end apartheid was Nelson Mandela.

___3.   Although cautiously optimistic about changes in the Soviet Union, Ronald Reagan refused to meet face-to-face with Mikhail Gorbachev as long as the Communist Party continued to exist.

___4.   Unlike the Reagan–Mondale campaign of 1984, the George Bush–Michael Dukakis presidential campaign tended to focus on straightforward discussion of the issues rather than personal attacks.

___5.   The effectiveness of George Bush's presidency was limited by his rigid ideology that prevented pragmatic compromise.

___6.   The Gulf War was initially popular with the American public, but support waned sharply as casualty figures rose.

___7.   Because Ross Perot split the Democratic vote in 1992, the Republicans gained control of the U.S. Senate despite Clinton's presidential victory.

___8.   The "Whitewater affair" concerned allegations that President Clinton had been sexually involved with a woman that he met while on a rafting trip in the Grand Canyon.

___9.   The annual rate of gross national product (GNP) increase was higher in the 1950s and 1960s than it was in the 1970s and 1980s.

___10. The U.S. birth rate began to slow in the 1970s and at the same time life expectancy increased, so the average age of Americans was noticeably higher by 1990 than it had been in 1970.

___11. Asians constituted the largest group of illegal immigrants to the United States in the 1970s and 1980s.

___12. In the early to mid-1990s, a majority of black children were born into single-parent families.

___13. The major riot in south central Los Angeles in 1992 was sparked by turf conflict between black and Hispanic gangs.

___14. The advocates of making abortion legal chose to call themselves "pro-choice" rather than "pro-abortion" in order to stress that they were defending the woman's right to make her own decision.

___15. Although Bill Clinton escaped conviction on impeachment charges, the vote was so close in the U.S. Senate that he became only a figurehead president.

Review Questions

These questions are to be answered with essays. This will allow you to explore relationships among individuals, events, and attitudes of the period under review.

1. How did the United States respond to the end of the Cold War and the disintegration of the Soviet Union? To what extent were the approaches of reduced military spending and increased world responsibility contradictory? Give examples.

2. Explain the fundamental changes in the nature of the American economy that were evident by the end of the 1980s. What technological and global factors contributed to the transformation?

3. Describe the remarkable demographic shifts that occurred after 1965. What were the immediate economic and cultural impacts of these shifts? What implications might these shifts have for twenty-first-century America?

4. Describe how the field of women's history evolved to a broader concern with gender as "a critical element of the explanation for many kinds of historical experiences." What are some key examples in the nation's history from the 1870s to the present that illustrate the viability of this historical approach?

Writing a Historical Book Review

Writing a book review as an assignment in a history course is designed to promote at least four important objectives: (1) effective writing, (2) substantive knowledge about a particular historical topic, (3) the development of a historical perspective and an understanding of the nature and use of historical research, and (4) an ability to think critically about the work of others. A typical summary "book report" can at best teach only the first two objectives. A critical book review goes beyond mere summary to inquire into the overall worth of the work. There are six steps to preparing a review of a historical work. With some modifications, these steps also apply to writing reviews of other nonfiction works.

1.   *Select a book.*
Your instructor may provide a reading list, but if he or she does not, you will find that locating an appropriate work can be a very important part of the learning process. Start, of course, with the Suggested Readings at the end of each chapter of your text and with the book catalog (computer-based or cards) in your college library. Check standard bibliographies such as *Harvard Guide to American History,* and try consulting the footnotes or bibliographies of other works. When you locate a likely book, give it a quick once-over. Glance at the table of contents and the bibliography, and read the prefatory material to make sure that the book is appropriate for your assignment. Ask yourself if the topic seems interesting, for you will probably write a better review if you have some affinity for the subject. Most important, talk to your instructor; he or she has read many books and has probably graded hundreds of reviews, so seek your instructor out for advice.

2.   *Determine the purpose of the book and the intended audience.*
The best place to determine both purpose and audience is usually in the preface, foreword, or introduction. What demand did the author intend to fulfill with the book? Did the author write because there was no satisfactory work available on the subject? Did the writer feel that he or she had a new point of view on a well-worn topic? Perhaps the author wrote a popular account of a subject about which previous works had been dull and dry. Ascertaining the author's purpose is important, for, assuming that the purpose is worthwhile, the writer should be judged by whether he or she achieved what he or she set out to accomplish. Also determine the audience for which the work was intended. Was the work directed mainly at professional historians, at college students, or at the general public?

3.   *Learn the author's qualifications and viewpoint.*
Find out the author's academic background. Is the author a journalist, a professor, or a professional writer? Has this writer published other books on related topics? Consult your library catalog; check *Who's Who in America, Contemporary Authors, Directory of American Scholars,* or other directories.

Viewpoint, however, is generally more important than credentials, since an author must be judged mainly by the quality of the particular work you are examining. A Pulitzer Prize winner may later write an undistinguished book. But many first books, often derived from the author's doctoral dissertations, are outstanding. Knowing the author's point of view, however, may put a reader on guard for certain biases. A Marxist historian will often write from a predictable perspective, as will an extreme rightist. Biographers are often biased for or against their subjects. For example, after the assassination of John F. Kennedy, many of his intimates, most notably Arthur Schlesinger, Jr., wrote biographical works. A reviewer could not adequately analyze Schlesinger's *Thousand Days* without knowing something about his close relationship with the slain president. Look for information on point of view in prefatory materials, in the body of the book, and in reference works with entries about the author.

4.   *Read the book.*

Read critically and analytically. Be sure to identify the author's thesis—the main argument of the book. Look for secondary theses and other important points. See how the author uses evidence and examples to support arguments. Are his or her sources adequate and convincing? Does the author rely mainly on primary— firsthand, documentary—sources or on secondary sources? Consider the author's style and presentation. Is the book well organized? Is the prose lively, direct, and clear? Take notes as you read so that you can return to particularly important passages or especially revealing quotations. Remember that being critical means being rational and thoughtful, not necessarily negative.

5.   *Outline the review.*

The following outline is only a suggestion; it is not a model that you should necessarily follow for all reviews. You may find it appropriate to add, combine, separate, eliminate, or rearrange some points.

I.   Introduction

   A. Purpose of the book

   B. Author's qualifications and viewpoint

II.   Critical summary

   A. Thesis of the book

   B. Summary of contents, indicating how the thesis is developed (Use examples. While this will generally be the longest part of the review, you should make sure that your paper does not become a mere summary without critical analysis.)

   C. Author's use of evidence to support the thesis and secondary points

III. Style and presentation

   A. Organization of the book

B. Writing style (word choice, paragraph structure, wit, readability, length, etc.)

C. Use of aids (photographs, charts, tables, figures, etc.)

IV. Conclusion

A. Historical contribution of the book (How does the book fit into the prevailing interpretation of the topic? Does it break new ground? Does it answer a troublesome question? Does it revise older interpretations? Does it merely clarify and simplify the standard point of view? You may need to consult other sources when considering this point. See, for example, the "Debating the Past" sections in your text.)

B. Overall worth of the book (Would you recommend it? For what type of audience would it be best suited? Did the author accomplish the intended purpose?)

6.   *Write the review.*

Follow your outline. Use standard written English. When in doubt, consult *The McGraw-Hill College Handbook* or a similar reference. If your instructor does not assign a standard format, the following style is accepted.

I.   At the top of the first page, give the standard bibliographic citation of the work under review. (Reviews seldom have titles of their own.)

II.   The review should be printed double-spaced on good-quality paper. The typical review is from 450 to 1,200 words long.

III.   If you quote from the book under review, simply follow the quotation with the page number(s) in parentheses. For example: "The author makes the incredible assertion, 'Jefferson turned out to be America's worst president' (p. 345)."

IV.   If you need to cite other sources for quotations, points of view, or facts, use a standard citation style.

You may find it helpful to read published book reviews as a guide to the preparation of your own review. Most historical journals, including the *American Historical Review* and the *Journal of American History,* publish many short reviews at the end of each issue. *Reviews in American History,* which prints longer reviews, is especially useful. To determine where reviews of the particular book you have chosen have been published, consult the *Book Review Digest* or the *Book Review Index.* Assume that your audience is college educated and well read, but do not assume that your hypothetical reader has in-depth knowledge about the subject of the book under review.

Preparing a Historical Research Paper

A research paper helps students develop competencies very much like those that are enhanced by doing a book review. One of the best ways to develop a historical perspective is to actually write some history, even a short research essay. In addition, preparing a paper gives students the opportunity to become more competent in research skills and in the organization of diverse materials into a meaningful essay. The suggestions that follow are of a general nature, designed to enable an instructor to adapt them to the kind of project that best suits the class. These suggestions are directed to students taking the introductory course who may be writing their first historical research papers at the college level.

1.   *Select a topic.*

This should be done with the advice of the instructor. Many instructors have a list of suitable topics to offer their students. If no such list exists, you should consider the following questions: (a) Will the topic help you understand the course? (b) Can a paper on the topic be finished during the term? (Students often bite off more than they can chew. It is better to select a manageable topic, such as "Lincoln's Veto of the Wade-Davis Bill," rather than one such as "Abraham Lincoln: President.") (c) Is sufficient material available to do an adequate job of research? (d) Does the topic interest you? There are, of course, other factors to consider, but if the answer to any of the above is "no," then the value of the project is lessened considerably.

2.   *Locate sources.*

Sources for a research paper fall into two general categories: (a) *primary material*—sources produced by people who took part in or witnessed the events being researched (letters, diaries, pictures, newspaper accounts, and so forth); and (b) *secondary material*—sources produced after the fact and generally written relying on the primary sources. To locate these sources, you should first consult a bibliographic guide, such as the *Harvard Guide to American History* or *American History and Life.* This will enable you to identify a number of secondary sources whose bibliographies give you more material (primary and secondary) to look into. You should also examine historical journals, particularly those that concentrate on the field into which your topic falls. You should read related articles, paying attention to the sources they cite, and book reviews, which will tell you of new works on the subject. Once a source is located, you should write its full bibliographic citation on an index card or in a form appropriate to your software. This will make it easier to organize your bibliography during the hectic days just before the paper is due. Consult *The McGraw-Hill College Handbook* for examples of bibliographic and footnote form. Most colleges have collections of primary material—on microfilm or printed—to aid students in this kind of research. Be sure to remember that you must give citations for material located via the Internet or World Wide Web just as you would those found in a traditional library. If the source is one generally available in printed version, such as a historical journal, provide normal citation followed by a notation that it was cited from the on-line version. If the source is only available on-line, cite the sponsoring entity and give the Internet or Web address.

3.   *Do the research.*

The research process has as many approaches as there are researchers, but until you develop the method best suited to you, here are some helpful hints. Begin by reading general accounts of the circumstances surrounding the topic you have chosen. For example, if your topic is "Witch Trials at Salem," read a general study of late-seventeenth-century Massachusetts. Then turn to the more specific secondary sources. (Consult the Suggested Readings at the end of each chapter in the text for background sources.) Take notes on index cards, one citation to each card (or the software equivalent). In this way, you will have notes that can be arranged in the order you desire when the time comes to write. Do not worry about having too many notes. It is better to have too many than too few, which would mean additional research at the last minute. Also, when taking notes, be sure to record the location (title, volume, page) so that you will not have to backtrack to find a citation. If you do the work the first time, you will not have to waste time retracing your steps at the end.

4.   *Organize the paper.*

If your research is done systematically, the organization of the paper will all but take care of itself. There are, however, a few hints that might be helpful. First, do not leave this to be done last. Even while you are pulling material together, you should be organizing it into a loose outline. This will show you where gaps exist and reveal which areas need work, and will often cause you to redirect your efforts in a more productive way. In this way, the process of organizing is ongoing, and so when the research is done, the paper is organized. Still, you should prepare a final outline just before you begin to write. This forces you to go over all the material once again, makes it fresh in your mind, and gives you the opportunity to make any last-minute adjustments.

5.   *Write the paper.*

Again, if the previous steps have been carefully taken, writing the paper is easy. The notes you have accumulated should be organized to correspond with your outline. However, be sure to pay attention to your thesis so that the paper will not be just a string of notes. Write a rough draft of the paper, with documentation on a separate page. At this stage, citations may be in an abbreviated form, but they should be complete enough for later reference. Beware of the tendency to overuse quotations. As a general rule, you should quote only when the actual wording is as important as the idea being transmitted or when "colorful language" spices up the narrative. In most cases, however, it is best simply to put the information in your own words and cite the source.

For general information on the use of the language, consult *The McGraw-Hill College Handbook* or another handbook used in freshman English classes.

6.   *Prepare the final draft.*

After the rough draft is finished and at least one revision has taken place, the clean copy should be prepared. Notes may be placed at the bottom of each page, at the back, or in the narrative, depending on the instructor's preference. The bibliography should be placed at the end of the paper. Other additions—title page, table of contents, an outline—may be included or omitted as the instructor desires.

By paying careful attention to the directions given by your instructor and by following the portions of this guide that apply to the project you undertake, you should develop basic research and writing competencies that will help you in many other classes.

Answers to Self-Test Questions

Chapter 15

Multiple Choice

1. b	6. d	11. a	16. a
2. c	7. d	12. b	17. b
3. a	8. c	13. e	18. a
4. e	9. a	14. a	19. c
5. c	10. d	15. d	20. b

True-False

1. False	6. False	11. True	16. True
2. False	7. False	12. False	17. False
3. False	8. False	13. True	18. False
4. True	9. False	14. False	19. True
5. False	10. True	15. False	20. False
			21. True

Chapter 16

Multiple Choice

1. d	5. d	9. c	13. b, c
2. c	6. a	10. d	14. a
3. d	7. d	11. b, d	15. c
4. a, c	8. a	12. d	

True-False

1. False	5. False	9. True	13. False
2. False	6. True	10. True	14. False
3. False	7. False	11. True	15. False
4. True	8. True	12. False	

Chapter 17

Multiple Choice

1. b	5. a	9. a	13. d
2. d	6. b	10. c	14. b
3. d	7. a	11. c	15. a, d
4. c	8. e	12. b	

True-False

1. True	5. False	9. False	13. False
2. False	6. True	10. True	14. False
3. True	7. False	11. False	15. True
4. True	8. False	12. False	

Chapter 18

Multiple Choice

1. b	5. a	9. b	13. d
2. d	6. b	10. d	14. b
3. a	7. b	11. b	15. c
4. d	8. b	12. d	

True-False

1. False	5. False	9. False	13. True
2. False	6. False	10. True	14. True
3. True	7. False	11. False	15. False
4. False	8. False	12. False	

Chapter 19

Multiple Choice

1. b	5. a	9. a	13. b
2. d	6. a	10. d	14. d
3. d	7. d	11. b	15. b
4. a	8. b	12. a	

True-False

1. False	5. False	9. True	13. False
2. False	6. True	10. True	14. False
3. False	7. True	11. True	15. False
4. True	8. True	12. True	

Chapter 20

Multiple Choice

1. b	5. d	9. a	13. c
2. b	6. b	10. d	14. a
3. d	7. d	11. a	15. a
4. a	8. b	12. b	

True-False

1. False	5. False	9. False	13. False
2. False	6. False	10. False	14. True
3. True	7. False	11. False	15. False
4. True	8. False	12. False	

Chapter 21

Multiple Choice

1. d	5. d	9. b	13. c
2. a	6. d	10. b	14. d
3. d	7. a	11. e	15. c
4. b	8. c	12. d	

True-False

1. False	5. False	9. True	13. True
2. False	6. True	10. False	14. False
3. True	7. True	11. True	15. True
4. True	8. True	12. True	

Chapter 22

Multiple Choice

1. c	5. d	9. b	13. d
2. b	6. c	10. b	14. a
3. b	7. c	11. d	15. d
4. c	8. b	12. b	

True-False

1. True	5. True	9. True	13. False
2. False	6. False	10. True	14. True
3. True	7. False	11. True	15. True
4. False	8. False	12. False	

Chapter 23

Multiple Choice

1. c	5. a	9. c	13. d
2. a	6. d	10. b	14. b
3. d	7. d	11. b	15. c
4. c	8. c	12. b	

True-False

1. True	5. False	9. False	13. False
2. True	6. True	10.True	14. False
3. False	7. False	11. False	15. True
4. True	8. False	12. True	

Chapter 24

Multiple Choice

1. d	5. d	9. c	13. b
2. d	6. d	10. c	14. a
3. c	7. d	11. b	15. c
4. a	8. b	12. c	

True-False

1. True	5. True	9. True	13. True
2. True	6. True	10. False	14. True
3. False	7. True	11. True	15. True
4. False	8. False	12. False	

Chapter 25

Multiple Choice

1. b	5. c	9. d	13. b
2. d	6. a	10. b	14. c
3. a	7. b	11. b	15. d
4. d	8. a	12. a	

1. False	5. True	9. True	13. False
2. True	6. True	10. True	14. False
3. False	7. True	11. True	15. False
4. False	8. True	12. False	

Chapter 26

Multiple Choice

1. d	5. b	9. c	13. b
2. b	6. b	10. c	14. b
3. a	7. a	11. d	15. a
4. c	8. c	12. a	

True-False

1. True	5. True	9. True	13. True
2. True	6. True	10. False	14. True
3. False	7. True	11. False	15. True
4. False	8. False	12. False	

Chapter 27

Multiple Choice

1. d	5. d	9. b	13. b
2. a	6. b	10. a	14. d
3. c	7. d	11. d	15. a
4. b	8. a	12. b	

True-False

1. True	5. False	9. False	13. True
2. False	6. False	10. False	14. False
3. False	7. True	11. True	15. False
4. True	8. True	12. False	

Chapter 28

Multiple Choice

1. b	5. b	9. c	13. d
2. b	6. a	10. b	14. d
3. d	7. d	11. d	15. a
4. d	8. b	12. a	

True-False

1. False	5. False	9. False	13. False
2. True	6. False	10. False	14. False
3. False	7. False	11. True	15. False
4. True	8. True	12. True	

Chapter 29

Multiple Choice

1. d	5. c	9. c	13. d
2. a	6. a	10. a	14. b
3. b	7. b	11. b	15. c
4. e	8. b, d	12. a	

True-False

1. True	5. False	9. False	13. True
2. True	6. True	10. False	14. False
3. False	7. False	11. False	15. False
4. False	8. True	12. False	

Chapter 30

Multiple Choice

1. d	5. d	9. c	13. d
2. c	6. d	10. d	14. c
3. b	7. b	11. a	15. d
4. d	8. c	12. b	

True-False

1. False	5. True	9. True	13. True
2. False	6. False	10. True	14. True
3. True	7. True	11. False	15. False
4. True	8. True	12. False	

Chapter 31

Multiple Choice

1. d	5. a	9. d	13. d
2. c	6. b	10. a	14. a
3. a	7. c	11. c	15. d
4. c	8. d	12. b	

True-False

1. False	5. False	9. True	13. True
2. True	6. False	10. False	14. True
3. False	7. False	11. True	15. True
4. True	8. True	12. False	

Chapter 32

Multiple Choice

1. a	5. c	9. d	13. e
2. d	6. b	10. b	14. b
3. a	7. c	11. d	15. c
4. b	8. a	12. a	

True-False

1. True	5. True	9. False	13. False
2. False	6. False	10. True	14. False
3. False	7. True	11. True	15. True
4. True	8. True	12. False	

Chapter 33

Multiple Choice

1. b	5. b	9. b	13. d
2. d	6. d	10. b	14. c
3. e	7. a	11. d	15. d
4. b	8. a	12. c	

True-False

1. False	5. True	9. False	13. True
2. True	6. True	10. False	14. False
3. True	7. False	11. False	15. True
4. False	8. False	12. False	

Chapter 34

Multiple Choice

1. c	5. a	9. a	13. b
2. d	6. b	10. d	14. a
3. a	7. d	11. a	15. d
4. b	8. d	12. d	

True-False

1. True	5. False	9. True	13. False
2. False	6. False	10. True	14. True
3. False	7. False	11. False	15. False
4. False	8. False	12. False	